Signs
of a New
Kingdom

Signs of a New Kingdom

3rd Edition

Seeing Even Greater Things Than These

Compiled,

Narrated,

and illustrated

by Ross Boone

SIGNS OF A NEW KINGDOM:
SEEING EVEN GREATER THINGS THAN THESE

Find related information about this book at:

RawSpoon.com/Signs-of-A-New-Kingdom/

There I have posted the videos of the interviews in this book.

Also, I would love to know how these stories touch you or others. Please leave thoughts of any kind in the comments section on that page.

And if you'd like the full-length audio files you can email me. Feel free to write me if you want to connect for any reason!

Contact me at Ross.Boone@RawSpoon.com

www.RawSpoon.com

Look me up on Facebook as Raw Spoon, on Twitter as @rossboone, and Instagram as rossboone.

I would love it if you wanted to take a picture of this book and post it on social media. You can say something like, "I'm excited to get Ross Boone's new book!" #RawSpoon

Watch for the follow up book in which I have interviewed Americans, looking for the type of faith I saw in Ethiopia, and then recorded how what I learned changed my heart.

"I tell you the truth,
anyone who has faith in me
will do what I have been doing.
He will do even greater things than these…"

-Jesus of Nazareth

There is no scientific evidence
that says God doesn't exist.

But there is ample
experiential evidence
that says that He does.

Dedicated to Richard Boone,
my uncle who gave me new life,
by giving his own.

TABLE OF CONTENTS

Preface

Structure of this book

This book tells about old-world miracles happening in modern day Ethiopia.

And it tells the story of how they taught my lame faith to stand up and run.

A lot of these stories get pretty weird, and although that makes me uncomfortable, I've tried to edit them in a way that not only makes them most readable, but also the most accurate to what I understand the meaning to be. For details, see the appendix on transcription.

You can watch video of each interview at Rawspoon.com/Signs-of-A-New-Kingdom/ or by following the links given at the beginning of the interview chapters. Seeing their faces and mannerisms brings a whole new level of reality to their unusual stories.

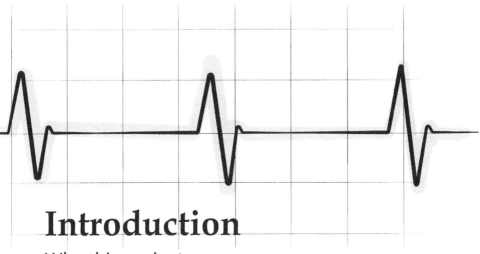

Introduction

Why this project

My dad has gone to Ethiopia every year for the past 11 years. He has poured months and months of his life into Ethiopia and he asks me if I would like to go with him almost every time.

And every time, until last year, I turned him down.

I just wasn't able to justify sinking a boatload of money into making the trip. He goes with a group that plants churches, provides pastoral training, and gives medical aid to the locals. I don't have skills in any of those areas and honestly, it sounded like I only had a fraction of the faith that the Ethiopians had.

He told me stories about how the Ethiopians routinely cast out demons, heal the sick, and even raise people from the dead.

I am just a writer/illustrator and I feel called to speak

to my *own* people, of my *own* land, in my *own* language. I write about trying to live out modern-day Christianity in an American culture that makes Christianity seem increasingly obsolete.

But the reality is that I too had become just a jaded, churched-from-birth, American skeptic who struggled to believe his own faith. Although I had gone to church religiously since childhood, I didn't feel like God had ever proven himself real to me.

I had fully earned my doubt and discontent with God.

But then last summer my dad's twin brother, my Uncle Richard, had a heart attack and passed away. That's when it hit me that my dad won't be around forever and I hadn't spent the time with him to see what he pours his life into. So I decided to go to Ethiopia with him on October 30th, 2014.

And after some creative thinking, I figured out something I could bring to the mission. I would search for, and record the stories of miracles and bring them back to my own people. I would bring the faith of the Ethiopians back to the people of my land, in my language, struggling to believe, like me.

When someone commented about all the miracles Jesus did, he said, "You will do even greater things than these."[1]

This is a book of finding just that.

---

[1] John 14:12

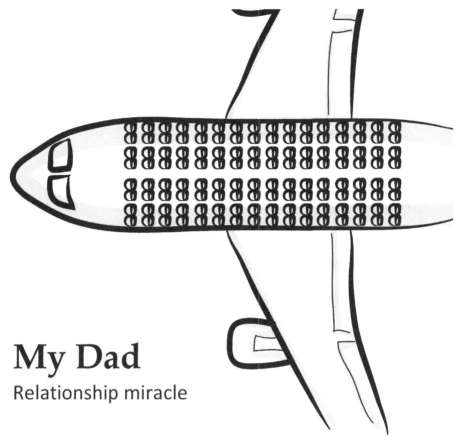

My Dad
Relationship miracle

My dad and I are very different. He is a great man, but sometimes we misunderstand each other and get hurt.

I am a freelance illustrator and writer, wrangling words with images to penetrate hearts and pull the most meaning out of life. He is a petroleum engineer, crunching calculations with computer programs to pierce the earth and pull the most oil out of the ground.

I am a sensitive feeler.

He is a strong thinker.

He has always taken good care of our whole family, and supported me in everything I do. He is a GREAT dad, but that hasn't prevented me from feeling hurt sometimes when our differences clash. Like when we didn't communicate very well during our last two phone conversations to coordinate for Ethiopia. After I asked him to repeat some logistical things a couple times I thoroughly recognized the exasperation in his voice.

He's learned that I ask a lot of unnecessary questions, unnecessary for a linear mind to ask. I ask for answers an engineer would have gathered . . . *the first time*. And because it happens often, it escalates quickly. And like we all do with ones to whom we are bonded we both tried to correct the error of the other with the tones of our voices.

After our last conversation, I was mad and hurt for almost a whole day. I found myself thinking, "Screw it. I don't need him. I can just keep acting friendly, keep my emotional distance, and not let this relationship hurt me anymore."

But I'm afraid I have done that with everybody in my life.

Maybe that is partly because up through college the girls I crushed on were never the ones who crushed on me. And my little heart crushed hard. So I know how much pain hoping in unrequited love holds; it makes it hard to hope in love again. Maybe that has something to do with why I'm 35 and like being single.

And maybe it's also because I rarely intercepted my dad's love growing up because we communicated our love so differently. Perhaps that starvation stunted my heart. That would explain why I didn't feel deep sadness when my mom died ten years ago. Nor when my uncle passed away this summer. In both cases I barely cried.

Hoping in love from someone is hard and I've learned through the habit of hurt not to do it.

But I only have one dad.

Only one parent left.

And I only have one life.

So I've decided to try. We're going on this trip and as we enter tight quarters, bump shoulders, and try to communicate well for the next 10 stressful days, this is the time to get down to the hard business of really loving each other. I will try to let myself love vulnerably. I will try to pour myself into him and the things he has poured himself into, and to receive the love he has always been trying to offer me.

I live in Atlanta and he in Denver. So we booked our airplane tickets completely separately from each other, only trying to arrive in Ethiopia at about the same time on the same day.

But as I waited for my connection in Frankfurt my dad showed up at my gate. It turned out we had the same flight together from Frankfurt into Ethiopia. That was convenient. But when we *By chance we had been seated side-by-side for the final 8-hour leg of our trip into Ethiopia.* compared our tickets I was in seat 33C and he was in seat 33A. That was serendipitous. When we got onto the plane, we found there was no seat B between A and C. We were sitting directly next to each other. That just might have been miraculous.

By chance we had been seated side-by-side for the final 8-hour leg into Addis Ababa, Ethiopia.

When I laid my head down to rest, he rubbed my back. And I did the same for him, which has always been the one love language we have in common, back rubs. When other voices fail, back rubs speak for us.

But sitting there, side by side, we also talked. The conversation was kind and patient. We talked about my work, his brother's passing, and about my younger stepsiblings he was raising.

There, sitting next to each other, talking like adults about things familiar and meaningful to both of us, heading into a strange, foreign land, I felt like we were more than father and son. Now it felt like we were also becoming friends.

It seemed God wanted to give us a glimpse of His power and kind providence by giving us that time together. It turned out this was just a small glimpse of His beautiful work He wanted to show us in Ethiopia.

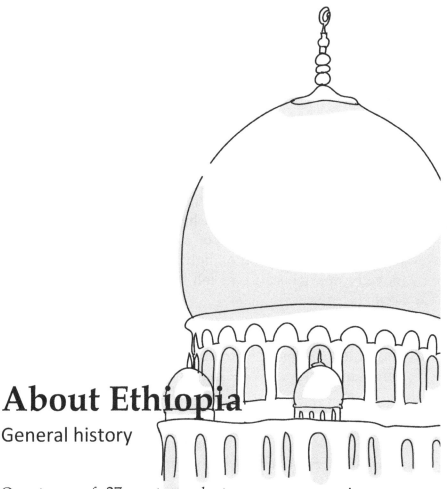

About Ethiopia
General history

Our team of 27 pastors, doctors, nurses, engineers, missionaries, and one writer/illustrator started in the city capitol of Addis Ababa. Our caravan of rugged Land Cruisers headed toward the property owned by the Petros Network in the rural village called Gojo, two hours away.

For each new church that they help to plant, they provide enough money to construct one church building, to financially support a pastor for two years, and to provide four pastoral training sessions to him. The mission of our trip is to bring American pastors to teach at one of these weeks of training as well as supply medical aid to the Ethiopian pastors, their families, and other citizens of the region.

As we left from the hotel in Addis Ababa, my dad said a prayer for our safety from the front seat and then turned back to tell us a story. On one of their previous trips a truck coming the opposite direction came so close to the vehichle that it ripped the door from a car in their group. No one was hurt but later, when they had arrived in Gojo, one of the pastors said he had woken up at 2 am the night before and had been moved to pray because he felt there was going to be an accident.

Ethiopia is a unique and strange place.

The oldest human's remains ever to be found were found in Ethiopia. You may have heard of her; her name is Lucy.

One of the pastors said he woke up at 2 AM the night before and was moved to pray because there was going to be an accident

Ethiopia is the only African nation never colonized by the Europeans.

It was where the coffee bean was first cultivated, thank you, God.

Ethiopia's language is not used anywhere else in the world.

Their bread, which is the main staple of their meals, is like a huge, spongy pancake and is called injera. It is made with a grain called teff, which grows almost exclusively in Ethiopia, partly because of its high altitude.

Ethiopia has a calendar all its own, in which our 2015 is still only 2007 for them.

Ethiopia is generally a peaceful country. There is not a lot of crime. And whether it is coincidence or not, Ethiopia was one of the first nations outside of Israel to receive Christianity. An Ethiopian Eunuch is recorded in the Bible to have talked to Phillip on the road to Gaza, and the Christianity he took back to Ethiopia with him grew independently from the rest of the world.

This specific sect of Christianity has become what they now call Ethiopian Orthodoxy and was eventually joined in the country by Catholicism and Islam. And now Evangelicals have begun spreading quickly through the region as well, partly because of miracles they are bringing. This is what I have come to record.

We saw spires of mosques and Ethiopian Orthodox temples poking between the trees as we drove through Addis Ababa. Statues of a regal lion donning a crown and scepter sit on top of monuments and gateposts around the city. The Lion of Judah is an image that represents Jesus and is commonly seen around Ethiopia, showing their Christian roots. In fact this lion was on an earlier iteration of their national flag. A country of competing religions speckled with relics of the days when Christianity was united and strong; it seems not entirely unlike America.

The Ethiopian Orthodox, Catholic, Muslim and Evangelical churches have historically been at odds with one another. But there has been a new movement in recent years. A seminary opened in Addis Ababa and many of the Ethiopian Orthodox and Catholic students started to realize that they had been neglecting the emphasis on Jesus. At first as these students spoke out they were scorned and even excommunicated but the ideas slowly became more prevalent. Now, in 2015, many of the Ethiopian Orthodox followers and Catholics are working with the evangelicals in unity, especially in opposition to the fast spread of Islam.

The indigenous religious presence, which the Evangelicals call witchcraft, is also very prevalent, especially in the more rural villages. And many of the Ethiopian Orthodox churches have been mixed with these lands' native, animistic beliefs.

Eastern Orthodox followers, Catholics, and people who were involved in witchcraft are often excommunicated from their communities after converting to Evangelicalism. But somehow it is still rapidly spreading. Evangelical pastors are planting churches quickly, and the growth is often triggered by the miracles.

(It's hard for me to think of any miracles I've heard of in America that would compel me to leave my family, community, and everything I know.)

This evangelical movement started in Ethiopia when the president of one of its nine regions asked an American pastor, Charles Blair, to sponsor 1,000 church plants before his presidency was up. Blair called up his friend, Ray Noah, as well as some other people including my dad, and together they raised enough money to plant 1,642 churches.

One of the pastors they trained, Bekele Godeta, moved to a distant village called Gojo and planted a church there but was stoned in persecution. However, he survived and wrote Ray Noah to ask for his help to plant 250 more churches in that region.

His village was Gojo, and the region is called Oromia.

At that time the region had 8,000 evangelical believers. But after working with Ray Noah and the other Americans for four years, by the end of 2014 there were over 200,000 believers.

This is where we are going and the work we will continue to do.

Church plant near Gojo

Prayer for sick woman doesn't seem to work

We stopped to see one of the church plants on our way to Gojo.

Our caravan pulled into a long, bumpy dirt drive. As we drove up to the church a group of Ethiopians welcomed us with a dance and song, hopping back and forth past us in a pack, drumming, clapping, singing and repeating what the translator later told us meant, "We will win the world through the gospel."

This church had been planted by a miracle. A pastor that Ray and his team had trained came to this village where there were no believers. The pastor saw a woman there who was possessed by an evil spirit, and who they kept in chains because she would stone people otherwise. He prayed for her and she regained her sanity. People believed his message because they saw this miracle and he began the church.

They kept her in chains because she would stone people otherwise. He prayed for her and she regained her sanity.

Since then he said he had seen so many physical healings that he couldn't even count them. He now had 270 members in his congregation and they had built this church building on their own.

They welcomed us inside and continued singing. I could smell the mud and straw of the walls and the cold dusty clay of the floor. The inside was dark with only a couple squares of light as windows. White-teethed smiles flashed in the dark, singing.

The church pastor said a few words and then Ray spoke. He told them, "Don't feel alone here. We support you in America." Then he asked if anyone would like prayer for healing and a dozen or so people came to the front and gathered in front of us Americans.

I had no idea I would be asked to pray for someone. And before I had time to prepare, standing in front of me was a woman whose face looked completely blank, like it had been drained of life.

The prayers of the others began to fill the room.

I put my hand on her emaciated, bony shoulders with

no idea what was wrong and prayed for a few moments. But I stopped, stepped back and began to repent. I did not feel clean enough to pray for healing. I felt guilty of my history of lust and impure thoughts as well as other disobediences. But as I prayed I thought, "I will try to trust that if God wants to heal, He can use an unprepared, half-righteous man like me."

So I stepped forward and put my hand on her shoulder again. But she took my hand and put it on her stomach. LOW on her stomach. It felt warm and bulging. Maybe she was pregnant? Or perhaps her belly was distended from infection or starvation? And then she moved it lower, just below where her belt line would be. I just kept my mind on the prayer and did the best I knew how to do. But even while I prayed for her she buckled over in pain and she braced herself against the wall.

After about ten minutes the room quieted. There was a farewell message given and the people filed out of the building.

But the woman sat down in the pews, appearing to still be in pain. I went to her as the last of the others were trickling out. I put my hand on her belly again and began to pray. This time she folded back layers of her clothes so there was only one layer between my hand and her belly. Two other members of our group, Julian and Joel saw us and gathered behind her, put their hands on her and also prayed.

When we left a few minutes later, she was still holding her stomach sickly, the life still drained from her face.

It wasn't until half a week later that we found out what God had done through us and our prayer that day.

Faye Feda

Resurrection and casting out demons

(Video of interview: http://bit.ly/1NF6Zb2)

Once we reach our destination in Gojo we get settled into a cement dormitory that is next to a church funded by the organization. The church looks more like a football-field-sized warehouse with plaster walls and a corrugated, metal roof. For all of our meals and meetings we gather in a building made up of a dozen or so rooms, connected in the shape of a square, facing an inner courtyard. The space in the middle of the courtyard is a tiled clearing and in it are a raised fire pit and a freestanding hut. In this hut is where I conduct interviews of pastors who have come for the pastor training and who will take a break to talk with me. Faye Feda is my

first interview.

We sit down in the hut while people move around us outside. The pastor, my interpreter, and I sit close together in three chairs, my video camera and audio recorder pointing at them. After we are settled and have exchanged pleasantries, I ask my first question. I've come all this way and I'm ready to hear about miracles.

What is the greatest thing God has done in your life?

The translator translates for him and then translates back his brief and direct answer.

One dead person came to life again.

Yes. This is what I came to find out about. I watch him explain the rest of the story to the interpreter, whom they call PK (this is American speak for Pastor Ketsela). The pastor I am interviewing, Faye Feda, is tall. He has receding hair, graying on the sides, and protruding cheekbones that make his temples look concave. Deep wrinkles climb his forehead and crow's feet spread from the corner of his eyes. His chin looks sculpted, strong and young. He wears a pink shirt, buttoned to the top and a dark sport jacket. His clothes are clean, when many others' clothes here are dirty and limp. He has a very humble smile and peaceful eyes. He smiles as he describes the miracles.

PK turns to me and translates the following story.

I went to a village to evangelize and I saw a group gathered, crying because a woman had died.

They were waiting to bury her until the rest of the family could be there and be part of the ceremony. She had been 25 years old, married, and had a child.

I asked if I could pray for her. They said yes so I knelt

down and prayed from 3 p.m. until 11 p.m. I stopped one time but the Holy Spirit told me to keep praying so I did.

Then I told the family to untie the dead body. They did and I checked for breathing. She had started to breathe again.

I went to open her jaw but I couldn't; it was shut tightly. But I gave her hot water and told them she was okay. Then I left.

I went back in the morning and she was sitting, alive with her family. She had asked what happened yesterday and her family told her, "You were dead, and a man came and prayed for you and you came back to life." When I told her it was I who prayed for her, she went to my home with me so I could teach her about Jesus. She said, "Give me your Jesus. Give me your Jesus. I want him." She prayed and followed Jesus.

"You were dead, and a man came and prayed for you and you came back to life."

His small mouth smiles slightly as he glances at me. I'm amazed. And a bit skeptical. So I ask deeper.

Are you sure she was dead? Did you check?

Yes, I checked her. Her body was very much cold, and they had already tied her up in a cloth. She died in the morning and I got there by 3 p.m.

I guess they would be the ones to know if she was really dead

or not, and if they had already prepared her for burial it appears they believed she was.

I wondered if his other stories were as unusual as this.

Are there other stories?

I have stories of four people who had lost their mind. They ran around naked and stayed outside all night. They didn't have a place to stay or anything to eat. They would just lie down in the mud to sleep and eat dung for food. They never came near normal people because they were so wild. People would beat them, and threw stones at them.

For the first one, after I finished a church service one day I saw him with stones in both hands. I said to him, "In Jesus' name, I ask you to throw away the stones in your hands." He immediately threw away the stones. I asked him to stop and he did. Then I laid my hand on his head and prayed that he would not go anywhere, but instead follow me to the church, and he did.

No one dared to come near him because he smelled so bad. I covered him in clothes from the church. Then I went and bought soap, took him to the river, and washed him. We went back to the church where I prayed for him and the demons fled.

Before I prayed he didn't even know where he was. But early in the morning after I had prayed for him I asked and he told me his name, where he came from and his father's name. He became normal again and we gave him enough money so he could go back home. He even started attending church programs.

The second story is about my brother's daughter. She

had lost her mind too. She would force her way into any house she wanted and would run the house members out so she could eat what was there. That was how she lived. I asked my brother to send her to the church so she could be free of the spirit. But our family said no. So she stayed outside. Hyenas didn't even touch her (which is unusual).

So, one time I brought a man to help me take her to the church grounds. I went to her and said I have a good lunch for you. We took her to the church but when we started to pray she began to beat and bite us. We found rope and tied her hands together. For three continuous months we prayed and the spirits would leave her but then they would come back. The village said if she gets free of the spirit we will come to church.

After three months God helped us and she was freed. Then I got her washed up and took her to her father's house.

I needed her family to confirm she was free of the spirit so I asked her to go fetch water and she did. After she came back from the river I asked her to prepare coffee for me and her family and she did.

I stood up in front of my whole family and said this is my God. You couldn't do anything for her. But my God could. This is the God that I worship and you should also. And I told them about Jesus. Her father and 12 family members turned from practicing witchcraft and received Jesus.

For the third story, there was a man from the village who lost his mind. I asked his family members to give him to the church. They said no at first but I kept asking and they finally said yes. Now he is a member of the church and farms to help his family.

And for the fourth, it was my uncles' son who had gone mad and was sick. I asked my uncle if I could pray for him. But they would rather he die than he become a Christian. They went to a witch doctor but he couldn't heal him. Then they chose to go to the hospital instead of letting me pray for him.

After nothing else worked they finally came to me as their last option. They brought him and I prayed for him. For one year I kept praying for him, having him in the church. And after one whole year he was entirely free. He had six children. He supported his family by being a farmer. He also sewed clothes. So he became able to send his children to school. Eight years later he finally passed away and went to his Lord.

He prayed for him for a whole year? It's hard to imagine how I could ever have this level of faith and self-sacrifice. So I decide to ask how hard it was to get there.

What has been hard for you to surrender to God, and how did you do it?

He leans over and stress gathers in the wrinkles on his forehead.

Even though there are obstacles we face, it stays here in the earth. So we have faith in God and we can face the challenge. Any problem you face, there is God. There is our heavenly Father so you can lean on him. Again and again even in the future I will surrender myself to God. I hope I will see more miracles. I prefer to die while speaking good news and praying for healing. Many sick people have become healed from my service.

Of course people have beaten me until I bled, and taken me to prison but God works with me. After I came to Christ I helped plant 14 churches. Even now I wish I could plant 400 churches.

I know the witchcraft. I know the Orthodox. I know all but one thing. I can't understand God himself. He is new every day. This thing is in my heart. Until I stop walking, until I cannot walk, or speak I will serve Him.

> *I know the witchcraft. I know the Orthodox. I know all but one thing. I couldn't understand God himself. He is new every day.*

I want this. But it still seems so unattainable for myself and, I think, most people in America.

What first steps can Americans take?

Brothers and sisters in America, a worldly thing is a worldly thing. It stays here. Try to look and see what God has for you and stick to it. As you can see, I'm old. Jesus used this old person. God can use a young person even more. So give your life, your wisdom, your energy to God so He can use you to do more.

And with that our time was up and we wrapped up the interview.

* * *

I was blown away. Someone being raised from the dead? Demon possession? This sounded like the New Testament. And I never got the feeling from him that these stories were made up.

However, a couple things about his stories unsettled me. I thought that if God was all-powerful and if he chose to heal, it would have happened in an instant. But instead it took eight hours to raise the person from the dead, and even a year to cast out one of the demons.

I wonder if the spiritual world is a lot more like the physical one than we think, but it just happens with invisible materials and invisible characters. I mean maybe sometimes miraculous healing really might take as long as physical surgery because cells are regenerating and things are moving back into place.

And maybe casting out demons can take time in the same way a siege to oust a tenant in a fortress would.

Also, I cringe because that story about tying up the girl who was possessed and taking her to their house would sound sketchy in America. I think here in America they would probably be convicted of assault for doing that. But still, the reason they were doing it was out of hopes to heal her.

It's hard for me to imagine a hospital volunteering to nurse an emotionally unstable person for free for that many months. But the pastor did. Even if we don't like the violence of binding someone, it seems like it was done out of love for her.

I also wonder if what they call dead is really dead. And if what they call demon possessed is what we would call mentally imbalanced.

I suppose whatever they call it, the proof is in the pudding. They had wrapped the girl up for burial, which means that nothing they knew to do could bring her back. But the pastor's prayer did.

And if the people they say were demon possessed were really eating dung and running people out of their houses, there were some serious issues going on. But whatever the pastor's treatment was, it was effective enough to solve them when nothing they had tried prior had been able to do it.

And I know this guy could be making up these stories and pulling the wool over my eyes, but I don't know; if even one quarter of his story were true, it would still mean God works in the world today. They seemed so detailed and real. And he spoke with such peace, enjoyment and humility.

I think I believe him.

Abdisa Duguma

Pastor that was demon possessed

(Video of interview: http://bit.ly/1U2B09O)

I rarely know when another of the missionaries will be able to leave their training and be brought so I can interview them. So I always have to be ready. Eventually they bring Abdisa Duguma to me. Again, I graciously greet him and we get seated in our little hut with coffee and the recording equipment. I don't know what to expect after the last interview. But I know we have limited time so after some brief welcomes, I jump right in.

How did you come to believe?

I observe him as he tells PK the story. He has darker skin than many of the others. He is humble, tall, and has an old, checkered, button-up shirt with a slight sheen and limp

collars.

PK turns to me and translates this story.

My family worships the witchcraft. Witchcraft gave me this name. After I was born I didn't drink my mother's milk. Witchcraft says a baby will die if he does not drink milk or urinate within three days. But if he does drink milk, there will be hope. This is how I got my name. Abdisa means hope.

But I didn't die like witchcraft said.

When I was 11 I went crazy. People told me I used to carry around a rope to hang myself or try to run into the river so I could die. So my family had to chain me down.

Until I was almost 22, sometimes I would be sick, and sometimes I would be okay. This was my life before I came to know Christ. I couldn't even control my urine. I would urinate on myself whether I was sleeping or whether it was daytime.

When the opportunity came I went into the military and served 2 years until the government fell down. Then I went to live in the big city of Addis Ababa where I was still crazy and did many crazy things. I used to rob people and even take their clothes. I could do whatever I wanted because I was a soldier.

Eventually I had to flee Addis because they found out I was a criminal. So I went to another place and this is what started my journey to knowing Christ.

About that time I found out my father had been found dead. Then my mother hung herself. The spirit I had was going on to the rest of my family.

One day when I was trying to rob someone's warehouse, lightning came and struck the ground. *Abdisa gestures to the ground in front of him.* It didn't harm anything, but mud got into my eyes. And while mud was in my eyes, I asked myself, "Why do I do these things?"

> *One day when I was trying to rob someone's warehouse, lightning came and struck the ground.*

After that I started asking myself more questions. When I would see a river I would ask, "Who created this river?" When I would see my fingers move, I would ask, "Who made them able to move?" When I would see mountains, apes, and monkeys I would ask, "Who made these?"

One day my friend and I beat up 50 people at a time. We knocked people's teeth out, and took one person's eye out. I had some sort of supernatural strength.

I got into problems again and again and I continued to ask myself, "Why do I do this?"

There was a lady in my neighborhood that used to sing songs and tell me about Jesus Christ. I used to tell her, you Christians throw money at the ceiling and watch it fall as if Jesus were doing a miracle, to draw people to you. I said, "You all become Christians because of what you can get out of it. You will get money and wheat."

One time she was opening a songbook and I poured water on the book. She said, "You are not a human being. You are a soccer field of devil spirits." I admitted, yes I am, because I knew I did these abnormal things.

A friend of mine read me a story in Revelation 13 about a powerful beast that came out of the sea and caused war. I started thinking about this animal and becoming afraid.

After that I closed my door, knelt down and asked, "Where are you, God? I know my parents' god is not God."

PK looks at me and adds parenthetically that it isn't usually appropriate for men to kneel down like this.

Well, one day my friend and I decided to kill a person who we didn't like. We planned to take him out to the bush and hang him so it would look like he had hung himself. I told the man "We will kill you."

But that night I went home and dreamed I saw a man with huge muscles in his arms and legs.

Abdisa gestures a large, open grip to show the size of his bicep and then again around his thigh.

He had a chest that looked as wide as your hands held out. I thought, "This is a mighty person."

I kept 80,000 birr (about $4,000) in my home so I thought this man had come to steal my money and I could not fight him.

So in my dream, the person stood 200 meters away from me but he took two steps and he reached me. He stood on my body, clapped and said, "Stand up! Stand up! Stand up!" But I couldn't because he was so heavy! Then the big man mentioned a verse: Ecclesiastes 11:9,

Which says, you men do whatever you like but in the last days you will be questioned for what you did.

Before this dream I used to go to Orthodox priests and they used to say, if you need protection, put your Bible in your pillow. So I remembered this in my dream. I claimed the name of God, Holy Spirit, and Jesus. I saw in my dream a big sword like lightning hanging from the ceiling pointing down at me. I woke up and saw nothing was there.

I ran straight to the church. I found a pastor and said I want to become a Christian.

So after I came to know Jesus Christ, he came to me and gave me a seed to sow because I had friends in the neighborhood.

I used to buy coffee beans and then sell them. So now, when I *bought* the beans I told those people about Jesus. When I *sold* the beans I told those people about Jesus. That was how I started my ministry.

One day when I came home from selling beans, there was a bunch of people there. One of the men said his daughter had died. I asked them when she had died. She had died at 5 pm. I got there at 7. I knew that Jesus called Lazarus from the dead, so I went to the room where his daughter had been sleeping and told people to leave the room. I prayed, "God you called to me. You came to me in the vision. Where is your power? Don't say no to this."

I prayed for his power and put my hand on her and prayed for her. When she came to life I took her out and showed that she was alive. They clapped and laughed.

When she came to life I took her out and showed that she was alive.

It's amazing to me that because the Bible says Jesus raised Lazarus from the dead Abdisa assumed he could do it too. They really consider what the Bible says as true and deeply powerful.

Another way I ministered was that I hired Muslims to work in my coffee firm. I told them about Jesus, invited them to my house and showed them songs. One day they invited me to their house in their village and that day 7 Muslims came to know Christ. I planted a church there.

Amazing. He continues right into another story.

Near the place where I was, called Bali, there was a deep spring. The people would kill oxen there as sacrifices for witchcraft ceremonies. The spring was like 12-15 meters deep.

Here Abdisa begins to talk more softly and tenderly, and speaks more with his hands.

Well, one day a girl was missing from the village so the whole village went searching for her. They found out she had told her brothers that "There is a house and people living down in the spring and the person who lives there has called me." They found her there. She hung herself by the spring. Then her mom hung herself, and when her dad heard this he fell down and passed away.

When I heard these stories I went to see this village. I had done some training with Ray Noah and he had given us pastors a yellow rope to put it over our necks. I took that rope, some olive oil, and three stones. After I poured the oil over the three stones I went to the spring filled with faith. I said to the demon in that place, either I will die here or you come out of this well. I prayed and threw one of the stones into the water. I took the rope and beat the water many times while speaking in tongues.

I left to go to another village to preach the gospel but after two weeks the water had almost dried up. There was a little left but it wasn't even above my knee. It used to be 10 meters wide, now less than one meter.

I'm not sure why the rope or the stones and oil are important but that sounds like something that would have been done in the Old Testament.

One time people called me because their cow had given birth but the calf couldn't walk. The people said if the calf walks we will receive your god. I said, "No problem, but first I must ask you a question: the witchcraft thing they gave you to have around your neck, will you give it to me?" She said "No, I paid 500 birr for it (about $25)." So I asked her which one is greater: 500 birr or your calf? She said she wants her calf, and she took it off.

So I prayed, "Jesus that I saw in my dreams, where are you? I pray in Jesus' name." When I prayed the mother cow came near, made a

When I prayed the mother cow came near, made a sound and the calf got up and went to its mom.

sound and the calf got up and went to its mom.

And then another story.

There was a boy who died because of a stomach illness and after three days I went there to tell them about Jesus Christ. I found the father was sick in the same way his son had been. I put olive oil on my hands and I laid my hand on his stomach and prayed. What this man had in his stomach came out as air from his butt, and as soon as the man stood up 22 people received Christ.

Nice. He saved 22 people by inducing a voluminous fart.

But the witch doctor of the village said, "Abdisa has to die. The person who kills Abdisa will get 10,000 birr (about $500) and a pistol." So, the next day, when I went back to the village to teach them about Jesus a tall man with a long jacket met me. I said, "I love you. How are you?" The man responded, "I do not love you. You will not make it through the night." But the man couldn't pull the gun trigger. He went back to the witch doctor and said I don't want the money or the gun. I don't want to kill him.

Please take your hand off my back. It feels like there is fire on my back.

I went to a place named Degoye, where I started to help farmers by taking their plow over and laboring for them. When a person came and took the plow from me I went to the main farmer and stroked his back and told him about Jesus. The man said please take your hand off; it makes it feel like there is fire on my back.

Abdisa strokes PK's shoulder to show how he did it.

So I preferred to stay in prayer for four days. Some Christians from the village and I listed the names of the village people and we prayed through the night. We would call out their names and say, "God is calling you!" We prayed that the person who doesn't respond to this prayer, please make them go crazy so they have to come to the church. After a week a husband and a wife went crazy and people took them to the church and they came to Christ. Because of this couple many more became saved.

It's weird to think of praying to make people go crazy, but I can see how sometimes we don't turn to God unless we're desperate.

Then there was a lady who came from Aruse. She was possessed by a demon. Her family took her to the hospital, then to the priest to get the holy water, everything they could. One day I went to their home and said, "Give me a chance." They gave their permission so I started to pray for her. Almost 20 people gathered to see what I could do. One man had a knife to kill me if it did not work, but if I saved her they said they would give their lives to Jesus Christ.

I went into her room. She was bleeding and crazy and she stank and nobody would come close to her. So I said to God, "You showed me yourself. You took me from being a robber and person who had gone mad like this. So you see her." I said in Jesus' name, and when I said Jesus' name she screamed. After she was set free I lay down and prayed. When I was done I went out of the room. When the person with a knife saw me he fell down. So I prayed for him. He received Jesus. So did the girl, and another person.

"You showed me yourself. You took me from being a robber and a person who had gone mad, like this. So you see her."

I am obviously blown away by all of his stories. And I had been thinking, as I listened, that it is like he is living in New Testament times. And I thought, "I have a direct line to talk to someone who deals with things very similar to what the people dealt with in the New Testament." So I began a new line of questioning.

What does it feel like to be demon possessed?

He looks at PK for the translation of my question, and then begins his answer.

You don't know you are doing what you do. You do it for pleasure but at the end you get stressed after you do that stuff. So being possessed by a demon is like you'll feel you'll be happy if you kill someone or see blood on someone's body, or steal, or do wrong things.

What does it feel like to hear from God? How do you know it is Him?

Even now I feel his presence. I feel fear of God. I feel He is touching me.

Do you feel it always?

Whenever I pray. Whenever I preach. Whenever I am in his presence.

I assume that 'being in his presence' means whenever he is doing something to engage God, like worship or prayer of preaching.

I was thinking back to his vision, and trying to figure out how those things were powerful enough to make such a significant change in him. I wanted to make sure I understood them. So I asked.

What did the sword hanging from the ceiling mean?

At that time I considered myself a hero and that made me not feel afraid of anyone. So in that moment the sword being there was saying you can do what you want to do but you will have to answer for your actions. It was saying you will either die or live. The voice was from God. You know, even today when I pray, if I see that vision of a sword that person will be healed.

Do you think the big man in your dream was Jesus?

Well. . . *Abdisa smiles* . . . Actually I met him three times.

One time when he came to me it was after a church service where a worship leader had been saying, "Jesus will come." I went back home and lied down on my bed. That's when I saw a vision of a man standing on a mountain. I saw him up in the sky.

Abdisa stands and touches his waist with both hands.

The upper part of his body was far up into the sky and was hard to see. I was lying down and could see the mountain. It was like 10 km tall. As soon as I saw him I heard the worship leader's voice in my ear, 'Jesus will come.' The man said, "The voice you heard from the leader was for me; I am Jesus. I came to be with you."

Immediately, he was gone from the mountain and I saw a ball, like a sun come to my house. There was a big tree and the sun came behind the tree and a voice came from the tree. The voice said, "Today I will make a covenant with you; I will give you the power. Everywhere you go you can win with this covering." That covenant that I saw was like a rainbow and the rainbow came down on my head. When I woke up I was speaking in tongues and disturbing all the people in my house.

My mind goes to the previous mornings when we had awoken in the dorms to the Ethiopian pastors praying loudly in languages we didn't know. Abdisa continues.

Another time I saw this man in a vision. It was two weeks after I knew Christ, when I lived where I used to live. I had a lady friend named Shitaye, which means "my odor." She had introduced me to my girlfriend whose name was also Shitaye. But my girlfriend had just died and now my friend Shitaye said, "Your girlfriend is dead. Don't be sad. Shitaye died but there are many other Shitayes."

And she said she wanted me to sleep with her. So at 7 that night I went to my sister's home (by where I would meet her) and Shitaye went back to clean up. When it was time I saw her walking back and forth outside, waiting for me.

I knew I had made an appointment but I couldn't get out of my chair! After about an hour I said, "What is the problem with sleeping with this woman?" I tried to leave the chair to go and have sex with her but I couldn't! When I was finally able to get up and leave the house I couldn't find her. So I went home.

Around 2 AM in a dream I saw a big fire and that same huge person in my house. He came and I saw a lamb. He had a stick and penetrated the sheep's stomach and took it and held it over the fire on the stick. Then he touched me and said, "This sheep is you. Before, you slept with four women. They were all HIV positive and they are all dead. But you are not dead. If you had slept with that woman you would die like a fire burning the sheep you see. I have saved you before. But if you do it again you will die like this in the fire. The voice said, "Live with me carefully."

The voice said, "Live with me carefully."

I didn't sleep with anyone after I was a Christian.

Do you think people who sin sexually can be used by God?

Abdisa takes a moment, thinking hard.

They can't be used by God.

This surprises me a little bit. I assume that this doesn't mean they aren't saved but maybe they won't have miraculous healing powers if they are living in sexual sin.

I wanted to know more about what Jesus was like in his dream.

What did Jesus' voice sound like?

Abdisa gets a big smile

I don't have a word. Sweet.

But he was commanding you. How could it be sweet?

Yes . . .

Abdisa continues to smile deeply.

The voice comes from Love. Every time I hear his voice it comes from love.

Abdisa continues with other stories he can remember.

"...and when I uncovered her face she was already opening her eyes."

I have planted 12 churches.

For the 11th, a church elder had a one-year-old daughter who passed away while he was away at theology college. They came to my house the morning after she died. I said the father must see it and ran with the child. But they told me it is okay; he went to study God. But I said, no he must be here! As I carried the child I said, "In Jesus' name" and blew into the mouth of the child and when I uncovered her face she was already opening her eyes and I gave her to her parents.

And he tells me one more.

There was a girl that was crazy for 18 years. I prayed for her and she was healed.

As our interview winds down I am thinking I have no idea how to bring what he does to our American lives, but I want to learn.

What can you tell Americans to help us do the same?

Have faith, depend on the Bible that he gave us, and do not practice it. Just do it. If you have faith in holy life there's nothing impossible for a Christian.

Why do you think God chose you for this?

Because we have His word and we are His covenant people, and because He helped us to be out of the darkness and we are living under the light of His word. I don't believe that God has done very many things in my life. He promised in Matthew 10 He would do even more things.

What is your vision for the future?

I want to plant 12 more churches, if God helps me, if I am alive. One of my supporters bought me a motorcycle so I could be free and go where I like. I used to show people videos on a projector, the Jesus film, but I can't pay for a generator and projector that I can carry on my motorcycle. I want you all to pray that for me.

How much would it cost for all of that?

Abdisa: 25,000 birr (about 1,250 dollars). One time I showed the film and I saw between 500-1000 people come to Christ.

As we wrapped up this interview and I wanted power like this I asked if he could pray for me, for freedom from my sins and power to do miracles. He did.

* * *

I wonder why Jesus appeared to Abdisa in the form of a strong man all three times. In almost all of the other stories in this book he appears as a man in white robes that is very bright. I wonder if maybe Jesus appears to people in different forms to suit the situation, like the people in the New Testament who didn't realize they were talking to Jesus as they walked to Emmeas after he died.

And it was interesting that even though Jesus appeared to him in a scolding way, the overwhelming emotion Abdisa felt was that he was loved.

I think I learned in this interview how important obedience is to God. He forgives, but then asks us to give up those things, like not sleeping with another consenting adult, even when it seems harmless to us. But maybe sometimes it is because, like in that situation where she had HIV, he knows something we don't.

And it was interesting that he said he thought those in sexual sin could not be used to heal people. It seems like it sets such a high bar for holiness in order to heal. Maybe we can't heal as often in America because we are often living in sin of some kind. However in situations like the next chapter it looks like God *can* use people who feel impure and inadequate, like myself, to heal.

And I want to use this to point something out. I've heard slightly different answers about some topics from different miracle workers. So I think this means that even though God uses many different people, if someone can do miracles it doesn't mean their theology and decisions are suddenly infallible.

I have a tendency to take their word as ultimate truth because God is using them so much, but I think I should remember we are always still humans. They are talking from their perspective and their experience, which is valuable because they have such powerful experiences that I would like to have. But someone else may have another answer that adds layers of understanding to it as well.

Woman's healing

I find out the woman was healed

Throughout the week we had a team of people to do short update interviews with each of the 272 missionaries who were attending our training. The updates were for reporting the status of their ministry to the Americans who supported them. Each of the members on our team was encouraged to help out with at least a few of these interviews. Usually four to six of our team were doing them throughout the day.

After doing a couple of the several-hour-long interviews, and while waiting for the next, I volunteered to do some of the shorter update interviews.

After a few of them, most of which involved healings and/or persecution on some scale, a man sat down with my new translator and me. He seemed to hold a secret behind his smile. I didn't realize why until half way through the interview.

He began by answering our spreadsheet questions about how his ministry was going. He said it was going well and he told a story of a woman who had a stomach sickness. She wanted to go to the hospital or the witch doctor but it was going to cost her 1,500 birr ($75). So instead she came to him. They prayed for her and she was healed. And because of it her family started coming to the church.

Then my translator spoke to me, "He says, do you remember the church you went to on your way to Gojo?"

I'm caught off guard. I recalled the church we had stopped off at, the clay hut with no lights and just a couple windows. The one where I prayed for that woman's stomach that didn't seem to be healed. The one where I had felt so unworthy to pray for them. The one I stopped in the middle to repent for my own impurities. How did this pastor know about that?

I looked at him. He was looking intensely at me, with a deep, knowing smile.

He said something and the translator relayed it, "I remember you." He said, "I saw you praying for the woman."

I was shocked. "That was your church?" The pieces fell together more. "Wait, that woman?"

He said yes.

And through a jumbled exchanged of excited translation the full story took shape.

This woman had been so sick that she couldn't come to church. He prayed for her, which made her healthy enough to come to church on the day that we arrived. We prayed for her that day and she had gone home.

She came back on Sunday a few days later for church, and told the pastor she was healed. And her family had come to church with her.

The pastor and I shared a long hug. Longer than I've maybe ever hugged a man. And we shared several long smiles as we were preparing for goodbye. It felt a little bit as if this man brought a message directly from God saying He was pleased with me. And perhaps to him I was like someone who had brought some of his family members to Christ. (I wonder if there will be a lot of meetings like that in heaven.)

He said, "You should come back next year and hold a revival at our church."

I was amazed and my eyes teared up over and over throughout the rest of the day. What were the chances that I would be the person who interviewed him on this very day? I only did about 15 of the quick interviews out of the 272 pastors over the course of the week. It seemed that God really had used me and the other Americans to help heal, despite my feelings of inadequacy and impurity. And how amazing that through it people started coming to church, and hopefully got to know Christ.

And it seemed God really wanted to show me how beautiful it is to act as His hands as they bring people to Him.

Girma Jabesa Dorsisa

Ethiopian miracles

(Video of interview: http://bit.ly/1NF7cLp)

Girma Jabesa Dorsisa sits down with my translator and me. I get him coffee and he looks into it as he stirs it slowly, and we prepare for the interview. He has a square head, and sits upright, legs together, like a child who is conscious of being well-behaved. His eyes squint often and appear to be watering. By this time I know to expect miraculous stories so I plan on asking tougher questions much sooner.

How did you become a Christian?

Well, my wife was worshipping witchcraft. My mom got sick and no one could cure her. Pastor Beckala came as a missionary to the place where we lived.

I remember back to hearing that Pastor Beckala was one of the first pastors in this movement.

Pastor Beckala told me there is no one who can cure your mom unless you read your Bible and tell her about Jesus. I said I don't care if mom is okay; I will believe. Then he prayed for me and I became a Christian. Then I went to the house of my mom and healed her. A demon left her. We realized it was a demon spirit so we decided we must seek revenge on the demons.

So when an annual national [pagan] ceremony called "falling half of the cross" came up, even though my whole family was celebrating I didn't participate. I stood up against this ceremony and traveled to each village telling them about Jesus.

So this is how I started ministering, by traveling to each village. The first thing I did was I went to my own relatives' home. When I mentioned Jesus, they tried to scream and harm people. It also made them fall on the ground. That day 66 people became free.

This boldness terrifies me. What would it be like to go to my family reunion and preach to them?

Girma starts to breathe hard and I see his eyes are still watering. I am wondering how exactly those people became free but I assume that they were demon possessed and he is too humble to say he prayed for them, and I let him keep going.

We tried to make a tent so we had somewhere to worship and I became a pastor for that congregation. I started a house-to-house fellowship. I started ministering, even crossing rivers and mountains, traveling long distances.

Some people came against me. The witchcraft people beat me and took me to prison. If I walked during the night they tried to shoot me. If I walked during the day, they tried to beat me. If I had to go to a village they went also and stayed there so they could kill me. But God would tell me to take another direction out to avoid them.

I started four house-to-house fellowships. If I couldn't go to see them I wrote letters about salvation and about baptism so they could teach. The village leaders came to know Christ through this and this helped protect me from those guys that wanted to hurt me.

One time I had a prophecy to go out from my home village and to go to the place where I am living now. I went but when leaders of this new place saw me they said, "This is a stranger who will destroy our community." They took me to prison for one day. When they asked to see my documents I said I only have a Bible.

After praying for one week God gave me a vision to plant churches in 4 places. But the officials said, "This man has come to harm us." So finally they brought me a person who had gone mad and was chained up, and said, "You have a Bible and say you are a servant of God. So let's see what you can do for this person." So I prayed for him and the demons screamed and said how they were hurting the man. This let the people see what the demons were doing.

By faith I ordered them to unchain him and I took him to live with me. He became able to talk again, and sing songs. So the people stopped opposing me because of this person.

I continued ministering and worshipping in that place. I had to find a place where people could worship the Lord so I came to the main church in the area. I shared my vision with the congregation and they raised money for me. Now I have opened six churches so people are coming to church.

He had downed the coffee I had given him quicker than the others so I filled him up again. He has a debonair smile and square jaw, with a sports coat and checkered shirt. He has receding hair worn short but has a young and innocent demeanor like a boy. And his head stays slightly bowed when he looks up to me with that peaceful smile. He tells another story.

There were two ladies who couldn't talk fluidly. I went out to minister and found one of them and prayed for her. She couldn't say a word before, but now she can. The other lady had a goiter so she could not breathe freely. I prayed, put my hand on it, and it went away.

I prayed … midnight until six. By six the baby's heart was beating.

One night people called me and took me to a place where a six-month-old child had died. I went there and checked and saw that yes, the child was dead. I prayed, "God we don't have a place to bury our dead. This is a place to express our faith. Please listen to my prayer." I prayed until six in the morning, midnight to six. By six the baby's heart was beating.

As he tells his next story to my translator, I marvel that this man just told me a story of raising a baby from the dead, and did it so matter-of-factly. As he tells another story to the translator, I look at the Bible he carries. It's an old, faded Bible, a makeshift paper jacket taped around it, and is stacked with the notebook in his hands. PK, the translator, turns to me and relays his next story.

In the small town I live in, named Galessa, people do not want me to stay in the town. So one time they secretly sent a group of gangsters to beat me up and do with me whatever they wanted. I dreamed that night of three sticks prepared for someone. I realized it meant they were already ready to beat me. That morning I went out to minister. They were ready, hiding to attack me on my way home when the sun went down.

So on my way home I met a man who said his son was really sick and insisted I go to his home and pray for him. So I went with him and prayed for his child. I found out it was a demon. Before, I had always prayed and immediately the demon would leave. But that night until 10 (4 hours) he still was not expelled. I asked God, "Why this new experience? I have never experienced this." But God used that moment because a group of gangsters were waiting for me. And because it took so long they had already left by the time I was going home.

So, early in the morning I saw a group of people carrying a person to the hospital.

By this part in the story he is smiling more, and is more and

more animated. He spreads out his hands in a wide gesture as he speaks.

After this man went home he didn't get better. Then he came to my home and told me all about how he and his friends had been trying to kill me. I prayed for him and forgave him. He accepted Jesus, and he went home. His whole family was saved and even now his daughter became a choir member in church.

I am assuming this man was healed because the man went home and was saved, though he didn't say it directly. Maybe it is indeed because he is so humble.

I have so many stories. Ten years of stories.

Then he tells PK something and PK tells me that now Girma wants to tell me his own story. And he begins.

God always protects not only my house but also what I have. Sometimes a disease comes through our village but none of my family members die. When something happens to cows, sheep and oxen, nothing happens to mine because of God's protection.

Many times a group of gangsters tried to kill me. If they didn't succeed, they tried to kill my livestock. They couldn't even kill my livestock.

If I don't get a chance to tell people about Jesus, I wait until there is a fight. Then I go between them and I act as if I'm a judge and I tell them about stories in the Bible. I use these situations to share how Jesus is the mediator between God and us like I am being a mediator between them. And I share how God and I are now like Father and son and how there is no peace at all without Jesus. I say He can set you free. The people start to think about themselves and forgive each other and love each other.

I ask him if he's tired and he shakes his head and says,

"I just open my mouth and God gives me words to speak."

I feel like I've heard enough of his stories to know God is using him miraculously. And I want to hear, from a man like this, the tough answers to questions Americans ask. So I begin.

Why do you think God allows suffering in the world?

He thinks for a moment and starts.

I believe God uses those situations to teach his people. For example God led his people to Canaan and they suffered on the way to where he promised. In the wilderness when they were thirsty and hungry, they were in good situations where they could trust God.

It seems this is the case with so much of this rural Ethiopia. They have to depend on the spiritual world for so much of their survival because they don't have other options.

The Bible says, I will lead you to the wilderness and speak to the hurting[2]. God leads us into rough situations sometimes but it's not because he hates us, but to teach us. Even sometimes God uses those situations for his people to let them see the situations as opportunities to seek God. And he uses it as a turning point.

---

[2] Hosea 2:14

For example, I can show you in my life. I know I feel God's protection when I serve him. One time I thought to increase the income for my family so I stopped serving him and changed my way. I sold Teff (the grain for injera bread). I expected and waited for the harvest time, but nothing came up to harvest. So I realized that my harvest was not this one. My harvesting place was the world of God and that helped me to know. So I came back to serving God.

So according to my understanding, suffering comes to people's lives to change their way of doing things.

Man, good answer. Let's try another hard one.

A lot of people in the USA think Christianity can't be true because it says homosexuality is wrong. What is your response to that?

I believe this is from demons. Because God gave his word from the beginning in Genesis, man cannot be alone so he gave women, and promised to have children to fill the world. So anything other than this comes from Satan. The secret things that Satan gives are against the word of God. They give themselves priority instead of the Word of God. If people walk away from God, Satan wants that, so he gives them a lesson so that when they come to the Word of God it comes against it and keeps them from coming to God.

I think of the people that will read these interviews that won't agree with him on this issue. But I hope they don't stop reading, because the root of his point is not homosexuality. I think it is that when we spend much of our time listening to voices other than God, especially from our culture, deep, powerful mindsets get built into our psyche. Then when we look up and find God's word is in opposition to our assumptions, we are apt to choose our own way because we have become so entrenched in it.

But maybe it is also important what he is saying about homosexuality, specifically. Maybe he does have a pure vision of Christianity not morphed by culture. This is a strong statement, but he is a man of strong faith, working strongly with God to make a lot of remarkable things happen.

As I ask him again if he still has enough energy to continue talking, he says again, I am not tired because God gives me words. I marvel at this man's faith and continue.

Have you seen heaven?

Yes, I see it from His Word. Every time I study Revelation and read John's story about the end after the world, I understand heaven. That's my understanding.

I'm amazed at this guy's faith. I need some help to even take baby steps.

Sometimes in our culture it feels like it's nearly impossible to jump all-in to faith like you have. What are practical first steps to get a little closer?

He looks worried as PK relays this. But then he dives in to answer.

They have to know that Jesus will come one day. But they must know that they must be ready. If they are not ready they must know he will judge them. They cannot escape from his judgment. He gave them his love and he will judge them because he has given them his love. For those who turn back, there is judgment.

What does that judgment look like?

Hebrews 11 says 'be strong in faith,' trusting His Word. We see God's men mentioned: Joseph, Abraham, and other peoples. They stayed firm. Your people have to be like them and stay in faith. Sometimes they can come to restoration. Maybe they have lost their faith, but there is restoration. God will restore it if He comes to them.

His straight forward, totally trusting faith simplifies so many of the questions our culture debates with the Bible. Whatever question I ask him the answer is whatever the Bible says. Could we let go of things deeply entrenched in us because the Bible asks it of us?

> *If you have a word from God in your mind, then obey it. Every morning if I have to go to ministry I pray and ask which person I should tell*

I think about the bold things you have done and I ask myself if I could even go knock on my neighbors' doors offering the gospel. How could I do that?

First if you have a word from God in your mind, then obey it. Every morning if I have to go to ministry I pray before I go out, and ask which person should I tell? Preparation first. If I need to fast and pray, I will fast and pray.

How do I know when I need to fast?

The Holy Spirit speaks to me, and the word is specific in my mind. I don't even think about other things sometimes, just the specific word. But there are also times God does not speak. There are quiet moments. Then you have a quiet time and wait until God responds.

But if you do experience having a word you have to somehow go out and speak it. Why would you prefer to stay at home?

Is there anything else you would want to tell Americans?

His legs are more relaxed by now. He gestures freely and smiles as he speaks.

If I die in the great commission there I have understood the great commission.

The mission you have started in our region, continue it and do it in other places. Be brave to do it day by day. Keep collecting finances. Keep teaching missionaries because we need to give the knowledge to ministers. If they have knowledge and capacity they can reach out more until we finish the great commission. Stay firm. My job is the great commission. If I die in the great commission, there I have understood the great commission. Without a church in a village there is no light. Because The Church is the hope of the generation. The peace and life comes out

from The Church. The good work God started in you
he will finish it until the end day.

* * *

I am challenged by how much Girma uses the Bible as
his answer to so many things. Has he seen heaven?
Yep, in the Bible. How do you fare well at the
judgment? You act like the righteous men in the Bible.

 He seems to know the Bible well and have parts
memorized. It seems like some of the problems in our
culture stem from not listening to the Bible. It is so easy
to first start with culture and try to add the Bible into it,
where it can fit. And not take the other parts so
literally.

And yet he also hears God simply in prayer. He asks
God who to help and he waits until he hears
something.

I am also impacted by how when you are following
that voice, it brings up resistance and offense in people
who will challenge or hurt you for it. This service to
God is not for the weak of heart.

I had found myself taking everything Girma said as
truth, but I have since then heard people who seemed
to be just as utilized by God say slightly different
things, so I'm learning that it is dangerous to make one
person's answers to be the whole gospel for everything.
We must test everything and decide for ourselves. But
these men have found something that works, so for that
reason they deserve a listen.

Thor Colberg

Miracles in America

Thorsen Colberg is an American pastor of a church called Vineyard North Charlotte and he came along as a teaching pastor on the trip. While I am asking myself the questions, "Why aren't these miracles happening back in America?" and "How can we make them happen?" I find out Thor has some experience in the matter.

We are finishing up breakfast on the benches just outside the little shack in the middle of the courtyard when I sit down next to him and ask him to tell me about it.

Thor, what can you teach me about miracles?

Well, John Wimber, founder of the Vineyard movement, would challenge us to pray for healing for 100 people. The implication was that we would see God heal. The reason we don't see God heal often is simply because we are not asking.

> *The reason we don't see God heal often is simply because we are not asking.*

Remember that Jesus only did what the Father was doing and said what the Father was saying. Our challenge is to learn how to hear the voice of God. That means, whether one-on-one or in home group or speaking to thousands, my challenge is to ask, "Father, what are you doing?" I can only do what the Father is doing.

Like one time, I was sitting in a restaurant in Colorado. I looked and saw the Spirit resting on a random elderly couple in a booth across from me. I asked, "Father, what are you doing with them?" Then I asked, "What do you want me to do?" I went over to them and said, "I feel like God gave me something to tell you."

They said, "Yeah, okay?"

"All your life you've been good with your finances. God wants you to know he's pleased with you because you've been good with your finances."

They got excited and said sit down and tell us more!" I said, "I don't have time now, but I'm a follower of Jesus."

"We haven't gone to church in years."

And I said, "Well, I think the Lord sent me for some reason to tell you that."

On another occasion, I was at a conference and am asked to minister to people. I prayed, "Show me who I need to go to."

I felt like God said, "There's a guy who's leaning against a column with a red shirt. He has three kids and his wife just left him." So I turned around, and sure enough there was a man in a red shirt leaning against a pillar. I went to him and asked the first pretty harmless question, do you have three kids? He replied, "Yes." Then I carefully asked, "I might be totally wrong about this, but did your wife just leave you?"

He collapsed in a ball of tears. I prayed for him and ministered to him.

This gets me excited. Maybe it is happening in America more than I thought.

What about healings? Have you seen any healings?

There was a guy who got out of a wheel chair. He had been in an accident. A small group in his neighborhood had been praying for him for a year. He was angry and wasn't a Christian.

When they invited him to their group he said, "I can't come. You don't have a ramp to your house."

So the small group built him a ramp and he started to come to the small group. And through that he comes to Christ. Then he starts to think, "God is going to heal me." His doctor told him, "Don't get your hopes up, it's impossible."

But one time, during a Friday night of worship his home group gathered around him and started praying for him. I was watching him from the stage and I saw his legs shaking. I thought to myself, "He's gonna walk."

His group members helped him up and he took three steps to the stage and sat down. His wife and daughter came running from across the room, so excited. They wheeled him out that night, but the next morning he thought, I walked last night. I'm going to take a standing shower. So he did.

When he went to his doctor he waited until she turned her back and he stood up. She wrote on the chart, "Miracle."

This guy was working at Circuit City and one time after he was healed he ran after a customer to give him the bag he forgot. I was there and said to the guy next to me, "That guy used to be in a wheel chair." The guy said, "I know, I come here all the time." I replied, "He goes to my church."

Have you ever seen any food being multiplied?

I had been thinking about the miracles and realized I hadn't heard one like that yet, even though it happens a couple times in the Bible.

Yeah well, we were feeding the homeless one time and word had gotten out so we had a huge crowd. We should have run out of food like 2/3 of the way before we did. But we didn't.

Here is a guy who's doing it. Maybe he has some advice on how to just really step into it.

How do you teach people to let go of their reputation and just do this stuff?

Wimber says, "I am a fool for Christ. Whose fool are you?"

That will free you. Let your reputation fall away.

The kingdom is already and not yet.

It's a paradigm shift.

I have heard people say things like, 'train people first and then send them.' NO! Send them out and then train them. When you send them first it develops a felt need for training! There will be a hunger on how to do it better. Then they'll want more training.

Show and then tell. Show how to do it, like Jesus did. He asked them to do it with him. Next, he sent them to do it two by two. And then later when they report back in he tells them more, teaching them about the kingdom, not just how to do it.

When they reported back in from going out two by two they said, "Even the demons were subject to your name." They are excited. Jesus' response is, "Don't get excited about that; that happens. Don't be surprised about healing and people being set free, that's normal kingdom stuff. Rejoice that your names are in the book of the Lamb."

How do you make sure you're plugged in to hear God?

Ask, "Father, what are you doing? And how can I take part in what you're doing?"

Don't say, "Bless what I'm doing." Instead ask, "Where are you moving, and how can I be a part?"

Do a lot of worship. Develop your secret history with God. Go to Starbucks and have a cup of coffee with Jesus. Put your headphones with worship music on and have your Bible there in case he tells you to turn to something. And listen to him. Don't ask for God's power. Don't you just want Jesus?

Some people ask, "Thor, how's your ministry doing?" and I say, "I don't have a ministry, I get to take part in the ministry of Jesus. It's His ministry."

Not one of you has a ministry. We get invited to be a part of His ministry. The secret of the kingdom is THE KING.

He pauses while I am writing, until another thought comes to him.

There is a difference between your calling and His ministry. He's our leader. We each have a calling, but we don't have a ministry. We get to take part in His ministry. And His is exciting. I want to be a part of His ministry. I want to be saying what the Father is saying and doing what the Father is doing.

As N.T. Wright says, "I'm a kingdom bringer."

Tesfaye Tesema Haylemarian

Ox comes to life after its throat is cut.

(Video of interview: http://bit.ly/1Lw3jc5)

When Tesfaye Tesema Haylemarian comes in we sit down, I make sure we all have cups of coffee, and we begin. Tesfaye has a sweater with buttons on the shoulder straps, which could fit in with my friends in the states, except that it's a little more worn; the wrists are stretched a little bit. He has an orange plaid shirt and a red undershirt that looks new. He has a blue ballpoint pen in his lapel pocket.

He smiles a lot. He has dark skin, and gray, lumpy whites of

his eyes. His buzz-cut receding hair is salt and pepper colored, as is his 5:00 shadow beard. His front four top teeth protrude forward slightly, separated from the rest. His upper lip almost touches the bottom of his nose.

I begin the interview.

Tell me about some things that have happened to you?

He begins by telling a story to PK who, a few minutes later, translates it to me.

19 years after I accepted Jesus I had a farm. I shared a river with the other farmers in the area for irrigation. I used to use the river for 24 hours at a time and that was enough. But the people came to know I was a believer, and when water was tight, they said you can only use it for 12 hours, which wasn't enough. So I went to the source of the river and prayed for the spring to have enough water for my farm.

I went home and after a while they came to my house and said the river overflowed and almost destroyed my farm because there was so much water. I needed to go and take care of my farm. So I went there and saw the river watering my farm without anyone's help. So I prayed and it went back to its place.

And here is another story. There was a tree standing by a big river. A live tree. The people worshipped the tree because it was big. They would slaughter sheep every May 1st. They would come together and worship that tree.

Tesfaye glances at me, I look at him and he glances down at my legs with a humble smile.

So I went to go to these people to tell them about Jesus because they were worshipping a tree that didn't mean anything. I asked a Christian friend if he could go with me and minister to them. He said, "No. If we go they will beat us." So I went to the forest and prayed, "Lord, they are worshipping a tree. They don't need this tree. I want to tell them about you." I prayed fire to come upon tree and be destroyed. And I went to a friend and told him you will see the tree dried and on fire. I went home and slept.

At night these people saw fire on the tree, at the top of tree. They tried to put water on it but they said that the fire just changed color when they put water on it. They couldn't put the fire out so it burned down. My friend heard their story and came to me and told me about it. I went and the tree was already burned down.

So after I saw that, I went home and praised God for answering my prayer. I went out again and tried to tell them about Jesus. Around 100 people came to know Christ that day.

I think of the big, beautiful ancient trees I have seen here in Ethiopia and think maybe it is a shame to have lost something so majestic. But then I realize a tree of 200 years is worth very little to God compared to his desire to be in communion with the humans He created.

Another story. My brother had an ox and one day his ox died in the middle of the mud. To preserve the ox meat they have to slaughter it and make the blood come out. So he cut the neck and let the blood come out. But since he was alone he could not pull the ox out of the mud. So he came to me to help him take it out.

I said okay. When I arrived his wife was crying because the ox means everything for them. They couldn't farm anymore. I said I will pray for the ox and he will come alive. My brother laughed and said I already bled it out. If this ox comes to life I will give my life to Christ.

I knelt down and prayed for the ox and when I stood up the ox stood up. And my brother came to Christ.

Then they fixed the skin of the Ox's neck with medicine, and a while later they were able to sell the ox for good money because it was alive.

> *My brother laughed and said, "I already bled it out. If this ox comes to life I will give my life to Christ."*

Tesfaye smiles wide again and as he tells the next story to the translator he points, puts his hand over his face, and then draws his hands together. PK translates the following.

We had a prayer group and one day a member came to me and told me one of the people passed away at 3 in the afternoon. This person told me to prepare him so they could take him to the burial place. I said okay and I cried and after I reached where he was, a verse came to mind. It was when the prophet Isaiah came to the king and said you will die. The king cried. When God saw the tears of the king he decided to give him 15 more years. I thought if God gave me that verse I must pray for him to become alive. I prayed for him from 3 in the afternoon until 9 in the evening. And now that pastor is here at the conference with me.

I must pray for him to become alive. I prayed for him from 3pm until 9pm and now that pastor is here at the conference with me.

Was he cold when you found him?

He was stiff and very much cold. They told me he died at 3. I reached there at 3:30. He became stiff by 9pm while I was praying. His mouth was wide. He was cold. But as I kept praying, at 9pm the temperature became warmer and I saw him closing his mouth. His eyes had been closed and he opened them and looked at me.

So after he opened his eyes and closed his mouth, we gave him food so he could eat. After three days I prayed again and cast an evil spirit from him. After a week he stood up and tried to walk.

In America when someone is dead for a time they have brain damage. Was this person the same before as after?

He is healthy and he is a minister in the church. He is here at this conference to get training with me.

I watch him as he talks to my translator. Lots of expressions animate his face at times, deepening the horizontal lines on his forehead. I notice a mole on a ridge at the top of his forehead. Sometimes as he speaks his voice quiets and his

expressions settle down while he tells the story.

Here's another story. There was a lady who hated me very much and didn't even want to hear my voice. One day she hid herself behind a stone when I was coming by and she slightly turned her face to see me. When she saw me she couldn't turn her face back. She couldn't turn her neck around anymore. It was stuck in that position.

He pushes his head to the side as if it were stuck that way. The whole time he has a clever smile.

So her child took her home and after a while the mom became okay. But the child lost her mind. The child ran away. Her mom went to find her and bring her home. But after her mom was running after her child her eyes became blind so she had to stop in the middle of the road. A person found her in the middle of the road and asked her what happened. She told her the situation and asked, "Will you please help me and take me home?" The person took her home and then found her child and brought her home.

Finally the mother didn't know what to do so she asked me to help. So I went and prayed for her. I prayed that the eyes could work again and I cast the demon spirit out of the child. Those two, and two other members came to know Christ.

It seems like demon possession is such a common thing down here. I wonder if it really is what they think it is. But maybe it is us Americans that don't know when we are possessed. Maybe in America it takes different forms. So I ask.

How do you know when someone has a demon spirit?

When we pray and mention the name of Jesus, the demon cannot resist the name and they will scream or fall down on the ground. That's how we know it's a demon spirit.

Do you have to say just Jesus or Jesus Christ?

The name of Jesus Christ. "In Jesus Christ's name."

Here's an example. One time I went out for evangelism. I went to a house and their father answered. I asked him if he would accept Jesus. He pointed to his baby girl, 2 years old. She couldn't walk. She had been lame since she had been born. He said, "If my child stands up and walks I will believe in Jesus Christ." So I had to pray for the child. I lay my hand on her and prayed in Jesus Christ's name and immediately the child stood up. And the father believed. So after they saw, the father and mom received Jesus as their savior.

Here's another story.

His face wrinkles this time as he's struggling to pick the right words for the story. Then he gets excited, and spreads his arms. My translator asks for clarification on something, as if it was unbelievable, and then translates for me.

There was a man who had already come to Christ. He gave me a piece of land so I could build a church but I didn't have wood to build. So I saw a really huge tree and I wanted that tree. I asked the man about it and he said I couldn't cut it down because people worshipped it. I prayed, "Jesus, I want this tree. Let it dry out this night." It didn't dry out but then I prayed, "Tree, uproot in Jesus Christ." The next morning it was uprooted.

These people took me to court because their god was uprooted. I met the man and the woman to talk to them about this issue. They wanted to take me to court and testify that I dug it up. But as soon as I heard them I said, "In Jesus' name let your mouths be shut." And they couldn't speak. So they chopped up the tree.

Did you get to use the wood for your church?

No, I didn't use the wood because they didn't want me to use it but I found another.

I couldn't help but smile.

Here's another story. And remember, I'm not telling you all the stories, just the main ones. There was a man who was a believer but his family wasn't. He sowed barley on his farm but what they sowed didn't come up. There were only a few stalks of it. Like, one, two, three, you could count them. His wife and son believed it was because people destroyed their farm. I went with a friend to the people to discuss. I asked if we could pray for the farm. He responded "No. Why pray? There is not hope."

The father, wife and son all said the same thing: "There is no hope for anything on the farm." I pushed them to pray and they said, "You can do whatever you want." My friend and I prayed on the dry farm. We prayed life on the farm.

After three months I went back to see the farm. It was full of what they sowed. But the head of the barley wasn't normal. It had a double head. Instead of one head it was double on the stalks. After they harvested it they had 1,500 kilograms. After that the whole family believed Jesus Christ.

The head of the barley ... was double on the stalks.

These are just amazing. I start to wonder if his prayers ever fail.

Sometimes do you pray and not see a miracle?

Yes, it is possible. There are times it doesn't happen. Even this year I didn't see anything.

Wow, as many stories as he has, it's amazing to think he hasn't seen any miracles for a whole year.

He continues with other stories.

One day a father came to me and asked if I could pray for his son who had lost his mind. So I went to his home and prayed, kneeling for three hours. I saw in a vision a three-headed spear was on his neck.

I told God I won't get up and go home until I saw the spear released from his throat. After three hours I saw the spears come out from his throat. And immediately the boy got up and he was healed. He's here at the conference with me. Also the man that was raised from the dead is here. They are both here and are going to plant their own churches. They are my friends and now they plant churches.

Thinking that it took three hours to pray away a demon makes me think that prayer, to a demon, might not always be an unlocked ultimatum, but instead more like a tremendous force battling or pulling or burning them. Maybe they hold on for as long as they are strong enough to. And maybe like

in the Bible a demon will respond to someone trying to cast it out by saying, "I know Jesus and I know Paul, but who are you?" And perhaps the bravery and righteousness of a man adds to the power, strength, and reputation in the spiritual world.

You seem like a godly man that doesn't struggle but are there times when you struggle?

Yes, of course there are times.

His face becomes somber for a moment as he describes some of it, then becomes animated again; so many emotions flow over his face.

Before I came to Christ I had animals at home: a horse, cows, sheep, etc. One day I lost them. When I came to Christ I had nothing. But I met a man who gave me 1000 burr ($50) to help. With it I went to the market and bought an ox and a cow and sold them at another market so I could earn a little bit of money and buy my own cow and ox, my own property.

After a while I became very sick. I was struggling with all these sicknesses, it seemed, except for HIV. Malaria and a bunch of the other sicknesses. I was very sick. A family member came to take me to the hospital but I didn't want to. They said, "What if you pass away? We don't have a burial place for you. You are a believer of Christ, so we can't bury you in our graveyards." I said I'd rather die trusting in God.

So one night when I was very much sick I remember praying to God, "If you want to take me now, take me. But if you want me to work for you some more take my sicknesses away." That night I went to sleep for the first time in a while. After a day I woke up and I couldn't find a single sickness in my body.

He smiles like he just shared an inside joke.

So a while after all that healing happened, I got twelve swellings between my legs, so I couldn't walk to minister to people. I couldn't even wear my trousers, but people kept coming to me, seeking my prayer. More than four people came and I prayed for them and they came to Christ because I prayed for them.

One lady came to my house to visit. I asked my wife to prepare some food for her and she said we don't have any food. When the lady left I asked my wife, "Why did you tell her we don't have anything? Look outside. Isn't all that God's? Aren't we God's? Everything God has is ours. You should have answered, I will prepare something for you." I told her to confess, and she confessed, "Forgive me. Everything You have is ours. It doesn't mean we have anything in our home, but we have everything."

I bristle a little bit when I hear the way he commanded her, but then I remember that the culture is different and the mastery of English is weaker, so it might not be as demanding as it sounds to my ears. But even if it is, it is direct and is encouraging her in her faith, and wants what he thinks is best for her.

So a day later a person who didn't know all this happened brought us teff and a couple of other food items. And another person brought us a chicken. Another woman brought us butter. Another person brought us barley and another milk. None of them knew about our situation.

I stayed home for two months. All those days people kept bringing us food. So I told my wife, "Look how God is working. This is His provision. It doesn't mean that we had or didn't have, but He provides."

He verges on laughing as he tells the next part. He points at the ground, perks his eyebrows, and smiles. PK asks a question and Tesfaye affirms the answer. He laughs at his own story.

One time after harvesting my corn I planted sugar cane. But thieves stole almost all of it at night. A little bit later the church ministers came to my home and asked to have some sugar cane to try it. I told my boys to gather the rest of the sugar cane. I said, "Finish it off." The church leaders heard me and asked why I said it that way. I said the rest was stolen. They told me, "Now, plant sugar cane again and nothing will happen to it." I agreed. We prayed that if any thief will try to steal it they would be caught. So I planted and when the new sugar cane came up my son saw a thief trying to steal it.

He ran after him but the man could not move or scream. My son caught him. People gathered and they asked to take the man to the police station but when my wife got there she said, "We didn't catch him; Jesus did. Jesus will do what he will with him."

We didn't catch him; Jesus did.

These stories have sparked an interest to know how he interacts with his family, knowing that often people who are remarkable in public can be hard to their family.

How does a man of God love his family, his wife and kids?

He rubs his chin and wrinkles his forehead while he speaks.

Once there was a situation in my family.

I came to Christ before I had my wife. But after we got married, my family and her family came to my house one day. They asked her to stop living with me because I was a Christian. They asked for me to give her half of my things and then to let her go. They gave me two weeks. I thought and prayed for two weeks. And they came back to discuss it. She stood up but couldn't say anything. But I said she is my wife; she is part of my body. I love her. I don't want to say bye to her. And she loves me too. So I won't give her anything. But if she wants she can take it. But if she doesn't want she doesn't have to take it.

Among the leaders one person asked me a question. "Do you drink?" I said, "No." "Do you beat her?" "No." "Do you beat her children?" "No." "Do you disrupt your neighbors?" I said, "No." The leader asked, "So, what do you do?"

One of my neighbors spoke up and said, "He prays to God." And so the leader said, "Then what is the problem? If he is a Christian, he can be a Christian. If he loves his wife, what is the problem? The love he shares with his children and his wife, let it be." Among the leaders they couldn't agree. And she stayed. This was the first problem we had with my wife and my family.

Realizing we had gone so long, I ask him if he is tired, if he

wants some more coffee. Both he and PK are ready for a refill and ready to keep going. I fill up their cups and then start down directions that are a little more tabloid.

Have you ever seen a demon with your eyes?

I didn't see with my eyes, but I saw one in a vision. I saw a spider making his web in the church floor so that the people couldn't stay longer in prayer. I realized the spider was like a demon and the web was like the works of a demon.

What do you think Jesus looks like?

Tesfaye looks as if he is about to cry for a moment.

I saw him in a vision one time. His shape is like a human but I couldn't see him because the light that came out of his body was so bright.

Was the light like a fire? Or more like the light from a star?

Like a fire. I couldn't look at him longer because it was so bright. Sometimes the fire was yellowish. Sometimes white. Sometimes like reddish. The chair he sat on had a bright light. His hair and his head are like a reflection of a light from a mirror reflection, like passing in front of a mirror that is reflecting the sun.

So you could see bits of his hair?

I couldn't see it for much time because of the light. Sometimes it changed the color to something like that green.

He points at our neon green nametags.

Sometimes strong light comes out of his eyes.

And in the vision I saw the book of life. It is a really, really big book. It has a reddish color. I saw a few other books, which were smaller, stacked next to it and I asked, "What are these books?" And he told me these books were the gospels, which the missionaries use as their guidelines.

The Gospels? Like Matthew, Mark, Luke, and John?

It was the whole Bible, on either side, in little books. I asked the man in my vision what they were. And he said, "These are the books of Moses. These are the guidelines for Christians on earth." I understood that the Book of Moses was the whole Bible, because Moses wrote the part with the Ten Commandments that were the instructions to the Israelites, but Jesus' life is the instructions of how to fulfill it.

What did the look of Jesus make you feel? Fear? Love?

Everything was perfect in my vision. The country was flat and everything was perfect. The light, the fire I saw, gave me joy.

Do you think you saw heaven?

I'm not sure, but that vision gave me joy.

He points to the sky and it looks like he is describing what he is seeing.

I saw my name in the middle of names after he opened the book. That brought me happiness.

Were there other people in the flat land?

No. And I don't want to add anything to that land.

Do you want to say anything else?

One time I had a vision and went to plant a church two hours away. I went to discuss it with the leader of the village. He said, "No you can't." Then another person came and she said, "You will never ever do this here. You can't even pass through this place." After a while that person became very, very sick and wanted me to come and pray for her. I went and prayed for her. But while I prayed, her mom, who was in another house, was possessed by a demon spirit and the spirit made the mother fall down. So when I prayed for the first woman, a spirit left her and she was okay. But I couldn't go to her mom's home because they wouldn't let me.

So I came back another time and the mom told the daughter's husband to kill me. The husband grabbed his strong stick and came to kill me.

I had a friend and we were going to check on them. But we met a man on the road and were suspicious so we said, "Hello, sir. Have you seen someone passing through this way?" He said, "I didn't see a man, no. Don't ask me." We said this must be our man. Did you see how he answered us? Then he came at us to fight us and I said, "In Jesus' name." And then he couldn't walk to us. One person saw him there with a stick and came to help us. But he found him unable to move. He yelled at him, "Why do you want to beat these people?" The frozen man couldn't even say anything. And we passed on and went on our way.

Later that person who had come to help us came and found us and called out to me, "Brother, I want to be saved." He said, "After I came to rescue you I went home and my father blamed me for trying to help. So I wanted to become a believer."

We went to his home and we cast demons out of seven of his family when we prayed for them and they came to know Christ.

After we finished that we met a person who took us to his home because he was very sick. When we prayed for him he started screaming and his ox outside started screaming too. So I thought the demon is working in both the human and the ox. He became free, and then the ox was okay too. After I prayed for him other people came to know Christ.

Do you think demons can be in all types of animals?

Yes, they can use animals. Even while Jesus was on earth he cast out demon spirits to go into some pigs.

As I hear so many stories from him of casting out demons from seemingly functioning people, I start to ask myself if having a demon is really as dramatic as I thought it was.

What are the other less obvious symptoms of having demons?

According to my knowledge and the culture I am in these are some of the symptoms of someone who is possessed by a demon. They will be sick. Their face is sad. While you pray for them they try to beat, scratch, run, or fall on the ground. They don't want to mention the name of Jesus Christ.

Do possessed people have special abilities in the spiritual world because of the spirits inside them?

He closes his eyes for a moment and then opens them.

Well, for example, when I was praying for a woman, I saw in a vision that something in the form of a dog went in and possessed her. After we kept praying the spirit left her. Sometimes the possessed can see things, but in this case she couldn't and I could. Demons are spirits so we cannot see them in real life, but in visions they are visible, maybe in the form of a dog or something.

It suddenly makes sense, that if dark spirits can help people see spiritual things, like possibly for psychics, so can the Holy Spirit help Christians to see spiritual things.

How do you be open to the visions? I mean, how do you make them happen?

So every time I pray I expect the Holy Spirit to speak to me. And the word of God comes and gives me knowledge or interpretation of something. For example when I was praying I saw a new sugar cane crop that had been eaten by something so much that it wasn't growing anymore. But then I saw a new spring of water coming up from the ground and the sugar cane grew again. I said, what is this? And I came to realize it means a new restoration of someone's life. Maybe mine or someone else's. It comes from *expecting* the voice of God.

Can anybody just start expecting it and it will come?

Yeah, if people expect God to speak to them God will speak to them. Sometimes God will give me a message for the congregation and I tell them and they receive their healings and message from God through me.

Sometimes people will hear their message through their pastors. Or maybe through the other people who are gifted in hearing.

Do you think that the people who can't do miracles are saved?

It's only the gifting. It doesn't mean they aren't saved.

What are some of the other giftings you have seen that minister to a community that aren't miraculous?

There are giftings of receiving guests. Serving people is a gift. Loving one another is a gift. There are others also. Cooperation. Teaching. Helping one another. Going to other villages and helping others.

Getting near the end of the interview and having heard so many of the other pastor missionaries' stories, my mind is starting to consider what bearing this type of faith has on how we live our lives in America.

What do you think of America?

Let me guess. I don't have any permission but let me guess. It seems like a clean country, having plenty of skyscraper buildings. You travel mostly by car and taxi and airplane and motorbike. You have plenty of education so you have knowledge.

Is that good stuff? Do you desire that?

If it is the will of God then I would love to see that country.

Do you want a life with more wealth?

Once I prayed, "If I had a lot of things but could not do Your work, I don't want that life. I don't want to have everything, but I will have you and serve you and die."

One time a rich person got my cell phone number from a person that I know here. And he wanted me to go to Addis and serve there. He promised to give me and my family a place to stay and everything I need. But unless God speaks to me I am not going to Addis. So I said no.

* * *

At some point on my trip I asked Ray, the head American pastor, "Why don't we see this stuff in the States?" He said, "I think it's because of the simple faith here. Even in the big city of Addis Ababa this stuff doesn't happen." But Ray also told me later that Americans and their money was partially why the ministry was able to keep growing so fast. His meaning was that since Americans have a stable economic system they are the funding arm, while Ethiopians with a stable understanding of faith are the miracle-working arm. We are functioning as different organs in the same body to tell people about God.

But I also am wondering if we can work miracles too, if we only had the faith.

I wonder if faith is so easy for them because their whole life is built on needing to rely on something bigger for help. If their crops don't come up, they die. If a sickness comes through their village, they die. Their only hope, many times, is the witch doctor that works a type of magic, or holy water that is said to have supernatural powers, or a miracle-working pastor. And so they are used to relying on the spiritual world. And when they find a spirit that is ultimately more powerful than any of the others, costs no money and wants them to thrive, they want to serve Him as God.

I also wonder if instead of miracles, maybe in America our developed knowledge in the hands of our peers is sometimes the avenue God wants to use to answer some of our needs. If I had children and they had learned to help each other, I think I would be much happier seeing them help each other because I asked them to than I would be if I had to step in myself.

I also wonder if in America maybe physical healing isn't what we need most. I think of the stories Thor told of being given a word to tell to the man whose wife had left him. Maybe the hearts of us Americans will be healed when we feel known. Known by people and by our God.

Judy

Seeing Jesus

It was only after hearing about what God is doing in Ethiopia that I started asking Americans why it isn't happening in America. Surprisingly, I am finding that it consistently is.

Judy is a quiet, middle-aged woman with short hair and a kind, round face. She is humble and peaceful and is quick to show her love to anybody who will receive it.

She was especially kind to me. But she became even more interesting when she told me she had seen Jesus.

Judy was married once. She said she did it because she wanted to be married and people told her she should take more risks. It turned out to be a risk she shouldn't have taken and it quickly ended.

She said she had always wanted to have a man that would just whisk her away on a horse. That's what she deeply longed for, a man like that, and when she had tried she had been deeply let down. Since that day she had been lonely.

She had been lonely until the day she was sitting on a beach watching the powerful waves rock back and forth. And she had a vision of Jesus. He rode by on a horse and swept her up. She never felt the deep need for a man again. In that one moment it had been totally fulfilled.

I asked her if she could tell me more about what he looks like and she replied, "He had white robes on. Clean white robes and a strong white horse. I couldn't see his face. But he so effortlessly swept me up off my feet."

"Could you feel his body? Or just the robes or something?" I asked.

"I just felt substance. It wasn't a bunch of robes. The way my arms wrapped around him, it just fit. It was just so natural. I think we were bare back on the horse."

"Oh and there was another time," she continued. "I had a dream where I was at a banquet with a bunch of people. I was with a man. I don't feel I've ever been in love before in real life, but I felt it there, with the man at the table. He was eating a fruit pie. He said, 'You have to stay here a while longer with these people.' He had a bit of the blueberry pie on his lips and I kissed it off. And it was just so sweet and intimate."

"Do you remember what he looked like there? Could you see detail better than the other time?"

"It seemed like he had longer, shoulder-length dark hair maybe. I'm not sure. I don't remember details of his face, except just wonderful. The feelings were intense."

"You just mostly remember the really wonderful feelings?"

"Yes." She sighs and says, "It was intimate. Just so intimate. Just such closeness. I just knew he was the person I was in love with. I mean madly in love with. But we couldn't come together because people were around. He said, 'Not yet. You must be with these people.'"

And then later she told me this.

"This is gonna sound crazy. But I was listening to praise music in my car one time and felt like I was suddenly with God as he was swirling around the chaotic void before the beginning of the world. And there was a loud voice like a resonant humming all around."

* * *

I don't want to have a religion where I look at Judy and judge her for getting divorced. I don't want a religion that is skeptical and questions if it is really possible that she was floating over the void with God before He created the world. I want a religion like hers in which my heart feels all of its longings are fulfilled in Him.

Where He is the answer to the deepest hopes I've always had and the most intimate needs of my heart.

It's kind of interesting that often when people see Jesus in a vision, the details are less about what he looks like, but instead that everything felt right. The fulfillment of their deepest longings were found in His presence and that everything finally felt like it just fit.

It's also interesting that Judy, an American from a culture on the other side of the world, had an almost exact remembrance of Jesus as some of the Ethiopians. He was so bright they couldn't see his face, wearing white robes, and they felt like they never wanted to leave Him.

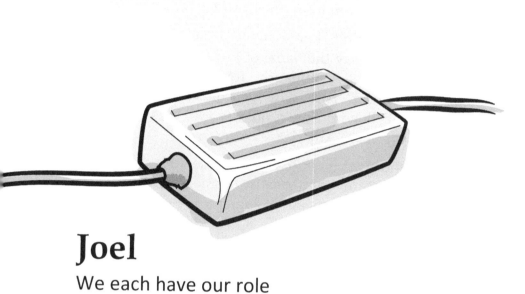

Joel

We each have our role

One day while the interview team was typing in the missionary pastors' stories to send to their supporters, several of the power adapters on the computer cords started smoking. Apparently there was an electrical surge that the circuit breaker somehow didn't catch and it fried the cords, making some of the computers usable for only the time they had left on their battery, even though there were days of interviews left to do.

As it was happening, Joel, our team coordinator, shot up and led the scramble to switch breakers and test cords. He had been an excellent leader for us and had kept things running smoothly so far.

But after having heard all the stories of miracles from the pastors, and seeing this as one in several circumstances that might be spiritual attack, my first impulse was to pray away the problems. Why was Joel stressing, relying on his own efforts?

But I also didn't know why I suddenly felt so embarrassed to say the name of Jesus out loud, like the pastors would have, and pray for this as people were running around? And why was it so hard, all of a sudden to believe prayer would work? This is what it feels like for me in America.

And I found myself confused and resenting the people that were scrambling because somehow they were embodying the doubts about something I really wanted to believe.

I looked around and Judy was coming near in her calm and unassuming way. She was one of the few I wouldn't be embarrassed to pray with. I asked and she said of course. So she and I prayed together.

But the situation still unsettled me. Is action the right thing or is prayer? When do we depend on God, and when on our own efforts? Do we Americans depend on our own actions too much? But would it be just as foolish to sit back and depend on God to solve the whole thing?

Later around the campfire I was in a group with Joel and he said something on an unrelated topic that happened to answer my questions, and it humbled me. He said something like, "We often look down on people because they have different giftings than us. We think because that person isn't serving someone, they are not spiritual. But instead, really they are a teacher, or something instead."

That was exactly what I had done. I had looked down on Joel for not being a prayer intercessor. And what he said was exactly what I needed to hear. He wasn't designated to be mainly an intercessor in that situation. His role was probably to try and fix the problem because he knew how to try and solve it. Maybe that is how God wanted to fix it, using Joel's mind and hands. Judy and I would cover the prayer.

I think that like different parts in a body, having different roles within a community helps to accomplish a goal better together. And I'm guessing our roles can shift. But it doesn't mean one way is the best or only way. I think we must be aware that God may call us to different roles in different situations.

> *We think because that person isn't serving someone, they are not spiritual. But instead, really they are a teacher, or something instead.*

I think this situation also speaks to how I have begun to see problem solvers in America. Maybe God sometimes uses problem solvers to be the method of miracles. I think as people attain more mastery over the world through education, technology and training, God will put more opportunities into their hands to solve problems alongside him, or under his guidance. For example, maybe healings by the skilled hands of doctors in America are just one method God uses to heal because He likes to see us becoming like Him. And He likes to see His children giving to each other.

> *Maybe healings by the skilled hands of doctors in America are just one method God uses to heal because He likes to see us becoming like Him.*

Also, I am seeing that this spiritual world doesn't have simple rules. You can't always just pray for God to step in and erase the problem. There may be other things that need to happen in the prayer for them to be healed.

For example, it turned out Joel has been part of praying for miracles a lot before and he told me a story where one time he was praying for healing for a woman and felt like he was to first ask her if she was dealing with any anger. She admitted that yes, in fact she was very angry with her husband, who was a pastor, because he was ignoring her to do church stuff all the time. And they had to pray for her anger and forgiveness before she could be healed.

In that same vein, Ray's wife, Linda told a story about some other strange little keys to powerful prayer and healing. She was at a women's conference in America and a woman was brought to her who was extremely downcast. She asked her and a few of the other women to stay after. She told the other women she had seen this before and she would tell them how to help the woman.

She said, "Sit directly in front of her and be aware that you may see her start to doze off. If she does, gently lift her head and ask her to stay with you."

As they talked they tried to get the woman to say, "Jesus is Lord."

"Yes," she would reply.

They said, "Who is Lord?"

"Jesus."

Now say the whole thing.

"He is."

They couldn't get her to say, "Jesus is Lord." And she wouldn't hold a Bible for long. Then Linda directed one of them to say to the woman, "In the name of Jesus, what is your name?"

When they did this the woman's eyes rolled back into her head and she dozed off. They gently lifted her head and tried again.

They asked again.

She finally responded, "John."

They eventually found out that John was the name of a man she was having an affair with. In this case John was the spirit of adultery that had taken root in her.

And they prayed it out until the woman could say, "Jesus is Lord."

I'm seeing that the spiritual world is as complicated as any craft or any kingdom when you start to dive into it.

I'm also seeing that diving into it opens up complicated feelings too. I would not have felt such hope, resentment, doubt, and then discovery if I had not stepped into the fray of fried power cords. I think we need to be prepared to be confused, let down, and do the wrong thing at times because it is a kingdom as complicated as the one we can see. But we cannot let those problems turn us away. Or turn us against our brothers or leaders if someone does it wrong. We shouldn't trust in any one person to understand the whole thing, and if you trust someone and they get part of it wrong, that doesn't mean that everything they taught you was wrong either.

If you trust someone and they get part of it wrong, that doesn't mean that everything they taught you was wrong.

In the end, we believe that God is bigger and that He is growing us to be like Him. It's an invisible world, and it takes more effort to get a handle on it. And since it is a very dynamic, complex one in which both demons and God move, there may not always be an ideal solution. Maybe it is a moving target so we must be ready to forgive ourselves and others, and then adjust.

It's also really complicated understanding how the invisible spirits come and possess visible beings in our world. Joel told me about a story from one of the missionary pastors he interviewed. This pastor at one point went crazy and went into the woods for years like

Nebuchadnezzar went out into the wilderness.

These stories make me think that these bodies are just a machine given to our spirits to live in for 80 years and it seems our spirits can share it with other spirits. We can allow things of our choosing to come in. We can allow co-pilots sometimes, and sometimes we can allow them to take the wheel. It seems like sometimes they even shove us aside.

But then I think that we, as Christians do want to be "possessed" by a certain spirit. It's a different kind of spirit. Jesus said he had to die so that he could send us *his* spirit.

And it seems the Holy Spirit is usually the type that only takes over after we ask Him, or allow Him to. I think He is probably polite and kind until it has to do with kicking the bad spirits out. Then He's like a dad raging on someone who has abused his child. And they fear him.

And once He's seated beside our spirit at the helm He lets us drive and whispers His instructions to us. And unlike most of the other spirits we can let in, it looks like He is always in it for our benefit. For the fashioning of our spirits to look more like His. The very spirit of Jesus.

Tesfaye Gadisa Ejeta
Prophecy

(Video of interview: http://bit.ly/1Jgrsjn)

Tesfaye has a break between his teeth, which are worn down from time but still symmetric. Red vessels blur into his eyes, and light colored cheeks sit beneath them. Later I notice a small birthmark behind his ear.

He has a humble posture and wears a sweat jacket. He has a five o'clock shadow, short hair, and is lighter skinned. He crosses his legs at the knees for much of our interview.

From the beginning, he came in with an inner smile that seemed to say he had a story no one else knew. I found out at the end that he had just seen a vision for me before coming

into our interview.

After hearing the piles of miraculous stories from the other pastors, I am assuming he has those as well. So I decide to try and cut short some of that in order to have time to ask him some difficult questions that haunt my generation. When else do you have an opportunity to ask questions of someone whose life actually looks like the life of people in the Bible?

We begin by asking him to pray for us. Then I ask him to listen to God about what stories and comments he thinks Americans should hear.

Can you tell me some of the stories in which you have seen God work?

There is a pause while he is thinking and PK suggests that we start with a story he knew about. "The one where the witch doctor's house catches on fire."

Tesfaye smiles very subtly and begins

While I was praying in my church there was a man of witchcraft who used to drink a lot and he would pass by the church often. So every time he passed by the church he spoke curses toward the church and toward the villagers in it. Sometimes he would kill black sheep and white sheep and do different types as sacrifices.

Well, every time I pray, I make this sound of "lelelelele" to praise the Lord.

He lets out a high pitched sound with a rapid lolling of the tongue.

But this man didn't like this sound. Every time he heard my voice, he would say, "Is there a newborn baby every day? Why this joyful sound? He doesn't work or anything; all he does all day is pray and make this sound." He always looked down on me. He saw me as less than a human.

One day I prayed and God said, "I will make him kneel down before me."

So I was away one day at a conference, but when I came back home in the evening and put things away my family members came to me and said the witchcraft doctor's home caught on fire and burned all up. They told me he had then gone out to my farm. So I went out to see him and he respected me now and told me this story.

"Last night lightning hit my home. I yelled for help but nobody could help the fire to go away. The fire just kept getting stronger and stronger. I told my family members to kneel and make the sound of "lelelelele," like you make. And while I did it the fire would recede. When I stopped the fire came back. From now on I will worship your God."

I told my family members to kneel and make the sound of "lelelelele," like you make. And while I did it the fire would recede.

The witchcraft man had three sheep to sacrifice for the spirit of his god, the devil. So I went to his house and knelt down and prayed to God, "Do you see what the witchcraft doctor wants to sacrifice to the devil?" God said, "I will destroy the sheep so he will come and give me the praise." In the morning I went and saw, and the three sheep were already dead.

That witchcraft doctor's wife got very sick one time. He and his adult son took her to Addis (the big city) but they couldn't heal her. They asked if I could pray for her. I said yes and they brought her to my home. And the sickness went away when the demon left. Eight of the family members were saved. Now I host a church at the son's house.

One day, I traveled a long distance to minister to the house in which I started the church before. When I got there, I saw Muslims around the house chewing chatt (it's a plant with drug-like qualities). They knew me and they pointed to a man who had been mad for a year. They said if you heal him we will come and worship your God. So I told them I cannot save. But I will pray to the savior and he will save, and you will see.

So that mad man turned his face toward me and came to beat and kill me; he tried to scare me. I didn't shout, but the Holy Spirit told me, "Reach out your hand and you will see what will happen." I did and said, "Devil spirit leave him, in Jesus' name."

When I called the name of Jesus Christ, that person fell down on the ground. I got courage and I kneeled down and put my hand on his head and prayed. He screamed and scratched the ground and the spirit left him.

Immediately after the spirit left him he knew he was naked and he knew he had to cover his privates. The Muslims who were watching were crying and they went home and brought the man clothes. There were 13 of them. One of the Muslims came a step toward me and said, "Your God is the real God and I want to follow Him. So I will stop chewing chatt." He took a drink of water, swished his mouth and spit it out. He raised his hands and praised Jesus. So after they saw him get healed seven others received Jesus.

Another story. Another village. There was a person who had been in prison for 9 years for killing someone and after he was released he was now in the village.

While I was ministering with people in a house I heard a voice outside the door. I heard someone screaming outside. They opened the door and the man from prison came in. While he was coming into the room the people in the congregation got up and tried to move him out because he was coming to beat me up. I told them, "Don't." I asked him, "Why have you come? If you have come to listen, please sit down and you will learn how to make your life better." The man reached to hit me with a stick. I said, "In the name of Jesus Christ" and the man's hand got stuck out straight.

Until I finished my preaching his arm was frozen, held out.

Here Tesfaye lets himself start to really smile for the first time.

As soon as I finished my preaching I prayed for the congregation and the Holy Spirit told me to forgive this person.

Tesfaye reaches his hand out from his side, and he looks in that direction as if he were speaking to the man.

So I walked to him and gave thanks to the Lord. I praised the Lord and said, "I have forgiven this person." Immediately he started to put his arm down toward his body and he asked, "What did you do to me?"

So I asked God why this thing happened. But the Holy Spirit spoke and told me, "Now his family members will come to you and will know Jesus."

That prison man's mom got sick and the hospital couldn't heal her. Finally someone told them to take the woman to me. I prayed for her and now she is a leader of women in my church. Three weeks ago that prison person came to me and got saved.

Okay, I've heard enough to know I want some answers on how to make miracles like this happen in my life in America.

What would you like to tell people who are scared to try to go do dangerous things for God?

Think not of your strength, not of your knowledge but think of the Spirit.

Praise the Lord. As Zacharias says, it is not by might, nor by strength, nor by power but by my spirit says the Lord. Think not of your power, not of your strength, not of your knowledge, but think of the Spirit.

If you see me I am not an educated person. I don't have a degree but I have the Spirit. Pray boldly. Give your personality to the Holy Spirit so he can use you.

What do you do when you pray, and someone doesn't get healed?

If I don't see a miracle I will fast and pray and take time. It could be days or months. I will take oil to the person and pray for the person. For example there was a teenage girl who couldn't walk. She was lame for 2 years. Her family members took her to one of the churches and they couldn't' help her. So her family carried her and brought her to me. So when she arrived at my home I started to pray and I realized that it was not easy. So I kept praying and I used the oil and put it on her body and prayed for her for three days. Then she was healed. She stood up and walked. So now she is a singer in my church.

After hearing that so many of the sick people had demons, I wanted to clarify.

When someone is sick, is it always because of a demon?

Not always.

Can you still heal them if it isn't because of a demon?

Yes.

Is the healing process different?

Yes.

What is the difference?

The process is like this. If a person is sick because of a demon, the demon spirit has to leave before the sickness does. And the person knows that the demon can still come back and take them again so they keep coming back to the church. And they keep praying to keep it away.

Those who don't have a demon might forget and stop going to church because they were healed so easily.

Then what needs to happen if they go back to their old life of sin?

Every time when people come to me seeking prayer for healing I will not directly go and pray for them. I will go to my room and wait for the Holy Spirit's response to know how to pray for the person.

So once when I asked God why someone was sick, the Holy Spirit told me I couldn't have him in the church while I preached because he doesn't live according to God's plan. So God sent the sickness to him so that person would come to church and seek God.

How do you know God's voice? How do you hear it?

It's not only when I'm preaching when God speaks to me. Anywhere God can release the knowledge. Sometimes I sit with friends and in the middle of conversation I understand what this person did before they came to be with me. They say, "Who told you?" I came to realize things so I knew the Holy Spirit was telling me about things like this. So sometimes they try to trick and check with me to see if I know what they did. So I tell them.

Tesfaye is looking at me more and more now, instead of the interpreter as he talks.

Even yesterday after our dinner we were talking with a group of missionaries here. I didn't know one of the missionaries; I hadn't seen him before. While I was talking with the others I saw him and told him,"After you finish you don't have to go home and pray for the congregation and for the sick."

"Why?" He asked.

"Because you need to pray for your family. Because you don't have peace among your family."

He said, "How did you know that? Yes, I will pray for peace in my family. I am even fed up in my marriage. I was thinking of stopping my ministry because of it."

And I asked him, "Your wife has a kidney problem?" And he said yes. And I prayed for his wife.

Was she healed?

He pulls a couple photos out of his hand. I don't know how or when he slipped them into his hand but they are a picture of the man and then another of the man's wife. He shows them to me with a smile. They are just little rectangles, small enough that the corners would just hang over a quarter- hers with an orange background.

Yesterday he called his wife and she was screaming because her kidney was healed. They invited me to their village to celebrate with them.

Also, there are a group of missionaries here that are sharing a room and yesterday night while they were sleeping I realized that one of the missionaries came here to attend the training and then planned to go back home and stop being a missionary. I tried to go to sleep but I couldn't. I went to him and said, brother you made a promise to yourself before you came here. Tell it to me. He wouldn't tell me. So I said, I will tell you. You told yourself you would stop being a missionary. He started crying. That missionary called his wife so that I could get the confirmation from his wife. She said, "Yes, my husband told me he would stop being a missionary and find a job to survive." And she invited me to their home so I can pray for them.

I see my opportunity.

I want you to speak over me.

Praise the Lord.

He smiles and looks sideways at me

Before I came into this room I saw a person who was filming. I saw God's hand over your head and this voice said to me 'God puts you on His hand. So you are in His protection and in His presence.'

At this point I am tearing up, making it hard to type. Something he's said has struck a chord. I don't even know what it was.

The enemies before you have put up something like huge, long ropes to make you trip. But before you were going to trip the hand that I saw over you stretched out a big stick so that it swallowed the ropes making your way become free.

I see a computer with my bare eyes on your lap. But I see a child in your hand.

What does that mean?

God said, "It is a gift I give him."

I will pray for you after this.

How can I care for this child?

He smiles again and looks down, playing with the pictures in his hand, his Bible with faded gold pages in his lap.

Well, for myself I saw that I was carrying lots of eggs in a basket. God wanted to see how I would carry those things. I was walking fast and one fell and broke. God said, "Why did the egg fall?" I answered, because I was walking fast. God spoke to me and said slow down and be careful with what you have so these eggs will hatch. You are the one to care for them.

As PK marvels at this message he mentions that he wants to ask Tesfaye to pray for him sometime too. I adamantly agree and ask Tesfaye if he sees anything for PK. He speaks for a long time before it is translated to me.

As he and PK talk I wonder why he rarely makes eye contact with me. He will do it sometimes in a way that lets me know he is not afraid to. But now I start to think that maybe it is because he is spending much of his time listening to what God is telling him instead. I think he is talking to us, but he may also be talking with God. Or maybe it's hard to look at someone when you can see so much about them, like it's awkward to look at someone when they're naked.

While he continues to speak to PK, I review what he told me about the hand over me and the stick breaking the ropes that would trip me. And the child he has given me to care for in my writing. And I think of the lives of all of these pastors I have interviewed. I think of the incredible stories that they have lived into simply because they listened to God's plans for them instead of their own.

And I'm suddenly afraid that when I get home things will go back to the way they've always been for me. But I really want to let these moments change me. I've tried to hold onto control for so long. I want to trust his goals for me, not my own.

It is so easy to trust right now. So easy to believe this and want this while I'm talking to the pastors who have seen it.

It is such a light feeling. And it is exciting. But there is also a little bit of fear. Like going into a battle not knowing if you'll come out alive. But also if I'm able to trust like this, even if I don't come out alive, I believe that all will be okay. These stories have eternal crossover. Every one of them seems more amazing than anything I've ever done on my own.

And I believe them! I think I really believe these stories. Even if only ten percent of these stories were true, it would still be evidence enough of a God for me.

Finally PK says, "Okay I will share with you what he said." But then Tesfaye says a little more and the attention goes back to something else he is saying. Tesfaye is making umph sounds, his hand in the air, telling perhaps how he was praying. I hear him mention his own name. I think this is a story of God speaking to him. PK says, "Amen." Smiles. Holds his hand toward him as if saying a prayerful yes, and says amen. Then shakes his head and gestures like 'wow.' "Amen. Amen."

Then PK tells Tesfaye's story.

I met a woman on the way in one of the towns. We didn't know each other. I greeted her and said, "You have a sore in your heart."

She said, "How do you know?

I said, "You are a Christian. You love God. But you have a sore. This comes because you don't have a baby. You put your hand to your womb and prayed you don't need a baby because of your tough living situation. But now that autumn has come you want a baby, but you haven't been able to have one. And because of this it has become a sore. This year you will have a baby boy." I left and after a year I met her again in that town. She said, "Man of God, we met on the street, and now I have a boy."

Then PK says that this is what Tesfaye said about him.

You are brave, you preach, you do good in the church but when you go home you fear. And it is okay.

"I don't even pray with my wife," PK tells me, and then he continues to translate.

But do not be afraid. I told my friends last night about you (PK), that you are afraid. But that God puts a big thing in your life so He can minister to others.

I didn't know about any of this with PK. I'm curious if the pastor is saying he needs to change, or just telling he knows this about PK.

Does that fear need to change?

PK replies to me, "Yes. Because I need to have fellowship at home with my wife." I share an understanding look with PK and then turn to Tesfaye again.

After a moment I gather my thoughts and decide to see if he has seen Jesus like the others. I'm curious if his description will line up.

Here's a new question. Have you seen Jesus?

Yes.

He gestures fast as if shooing a fly with his hand.

Once a group of people in my congregation came against me and it broke my heart. I didn't want to come to my pastor to ask for help. So I prayed for a solution. I went into the church, took off my clothes, lied down, and started to pray. And when I was praying I fell asleep. In my dream I saw myself running and running and running. And finally I reached a gate. It was beautiful inside. I went through the gate, and reached another one, also beautiful, then a third, also a huge gate that was beautiful. I heard a voice that said, "Son, why are you running? Why are you naked?" I said, "Things in the church are not good. If you tell me to stop I will. If you tell me to keep ministering I will."

I wanted to see the person whose voice it was. I wanted to know who it was. But I couldn't because the light was so bright. I said again, "I can't stay in the church because the situation is hard." But the voice said, "No, I gave you that church. I want you to stay there." I tried to look again but couldn't see him because he was so bright. I saw fire from the voice come and catch the back of my seat on fire. And I heard the voice next to my ear and it told me to stay with my church. I woke up but fell asleep a couple more times, each time having the same vision. Then I woke up and put my clothes on. I stayed in the ministry. So that was the vision of Jesus, full of light.

What did his voice sound like?

It was like a vibrating sound. Big. Scary. But it had like a tender tone to the voice.

One day I saw a vision of Jesus coming toward me sitting on a donkey. There was a cloud that was between Jesus and the donkey. And there was a fire beside the cloud. The donkey was walking on leaves. Jesus thrust a metal thing into the ground and told me,

"No one will touch this thing because I have planted it here." And immediately I saw him going into the sky like fire. I woke up and went to that place where I had seen Jesus put the thing in the ground and planted a church there.

Tell me more about what he looked like so I could recognize him if I saw him.

He's like shining. He shines.

What color of shining?

White.

Does he have a smell?

Yes, he does, but I cannot describe it. It is really pleasant to keep smelling.

Is there some sort of sensation he gives on the skin?

Yes. I'll tell you a story about when I felt him. Once I had a friend in the church. We promised each other that if I were to fall he would lift me up, and be with me and encourage me, and I would do the same for him. We kept this covenant between us. After a while, I don't know what happened to him, but he didn't want me to be part of the church anymore.

It felt like an oil was getting into each of my body parts.

Then I had a vision. In the vision was a deep hole that my friend had dug. It was behind me and my friend came in front of me and said, 'I love you, brother.' But he wanted to push me into the hole and bury me in it. I saw a hand come from above and he said, 'Give me your hand. Son, I am now here. You didn't know what these guys wanted to do to you, but I came to you.'

This hand touched my shoulder. It felt like oil was getting into each of my body parts. He took me with his hand and placed me some other places so I wouldn't fall into the ground and I still felt his hand as he put me in different places.

Was the hand and the oil warm, or electric, or what?

I felt happy. I felt energetic inside.

The next morning I realized that my friend had put together six points of which to accuse me in front of the elders in the church. So he said, "The church elders need us to be in a meeting. Lets go together." I said okay but before we went I invited him to sit beside me as I washed my hands and I told him, "Brother Nagash, someone came to me this morning and told me something. Did you know that? Do you know what they told me?"

"No," he said.

So I said, "Nagash, we had a covenant between us. Those people who were with you told me what you have prepared to accuse me of."

Nagash replied, "Did they tell you they have been pushing me to do this?! They used me!" He started screaming and shouting.

But we went together to the church and then to the pastor's office and Nagash reported to the pastor that all the accusations were lies and the pastor took the list and burned it. And they ordered Nagash to stop ministering in the church.

Are you guys still friends?

He is here at the missionary training with me and we are friends.

So you twisted the truth?

I just wanted to check whether he spoke the truth or not. This is the way to make him confess. Then I told him the vision and everything.

Is this an example of being clever like a serpent (Matthew 10:16)?

Yes. Now we are friends. We serve together. I love him so much.

How do you feel? Do you want to keep answering my questions?

Tesfaye smiles, nods, and is silent for a moment, picking his nose. Must be a cultural thing.

Just a few more minutes but now I have a question for you, Ross. Is there a group of people that does not worship God?

There are a lot of groups that don't worship God. I feel like a lot of people I know sort of worship God. Not with their full heart.

I think there is a group of people that think they are Christian but they haven't fully decided. They walk on two roads. I see lots of people behind you. When they come together with you they act like Christians and when they are apart from you they don't act like that. And you don't know why they do this.

I see this group of people is putting an obstacle before you.

Here is an experience of mine. When I went to minister at a house one time, people dug a hole and put a trap for my legs in it. After I finished ministering in that house, the Holy Spirit told me to go a different way home. Those guys who put an obstacle for me were drinking alcohol somewhere and after they finished drinking one of those guys had to go that way, and the trap got him. So that person got his leg wounded, and he couldn't even walk.

So Ross, that group of individuals is putting something in the way to harm you, but it can't get you. They will harm themselves.

What do I do to help them?

Pray for them.

Will they be saved?

Yes.

Will I see a lot of persecution?

No.

This is amazing. I want to know more about my role in writing.

Writing books is a way I want to reach these people with one foot on one path and one foot on another. Do you have a message for me about writing books?

This group of people worshipping with me here are not simply the ones that come to my church. They are the ones that threw stones at me, who cursed me, who mocked me. When they did this I went to their homes and to church and prayed for them. I prayed for them and even sometimes they saw a vision so that they found Jesus Christ as their savior, and now they are with me as my friends and people I minister with. So those people around you will come to Christ.

I think of my ministry as being two parts. The way I interact with people, but also how I make books. Should I make one more important than the other?

He rubs his chin, mutters something just loud enough to be heard and PK translates.

It is true; praise the Lord. I see two things over your heart. I see lots of books on your right hand. I see few books on your left hand. But God is speaking to you to seek His face first.

I assume that he is saying that the few books in one hand represent the way I interact with people, and the books I will write are the big stack of books in the other. But I'm curious which is which.

What are the few books in my left hand?

These books on your left hand are what you will give to those individuals with one foot in each path.

I'm still wondering if he means they are the books I will write or they are symbolic of my interactions with people. His answer was unclear.

What is the bunch of books in my right hand, then?

They are the word of God.

And I realize how selfish I have been. I have been worried about whether my writing or personal interactions were more important. He was saying that both of those only represent a few books. But the overwhelming majority of the books in my

life need to be the books of the Bible.

I ask Tesfaye to pray for me and the translator, PK. And in his prayer he prophesies even more over us. It was encouraging but this message is best only for us, I think. So kindly forgive me if I do not record it here.

And then I ask him what he needs, what we can pray for him. He says there is a large distance between the churches to which he needs to travel, and there are Muslims in between. The distance is hard. He also asks for six Bibles in certain native languages. We pray for him and organize the Bibles to be given to him.

* * *

This has been monumental for me. I have heard his stories, and the miracles that have come from him prophesying over people. And I believed them. But then he prophesied over me. It's like I can suddenly see my normal life through the same lens as I have seen the foreign, exotic miracles in Ethiopia. It feels like a validation that I can take this life of faith back to America with me. I have been called to rely on God as much as they do and depend on Him to draw people to himself like the missionaries do.

Alayu Kebede

Local leader of the Petros Network

(Video of interview: http://bit.ly/1JfvM04)

Alayu is a short man that usually wears plain, white Reebok tennis shoes. He has dark skin, like glistening chocolate. A youthful smile is always close to his lips. He always seems comfortable in his own skin. He usually wears a checkered shirt tucked into his jeans.

He is the national that is in charge of the entire program. When I first got to talk to him, standing in the courtyard he said, "How is your brother?"

"Oh you remember my brother?!" I replied, surprised he had remembered that he had come with my dad several years ago. "He's good."

"Yes. I remember him. I had good conversations with him. He reminds me of your mom."

"You remember my mom too?!"

My mother had come to Ethiopia with my dad in the first years of the mission. In fact she had been the first American woman to travel over to Ethiopia with the Petros Network.

"Of course I do." He said. "She helped us out for two years. I see her in both of you. Your dad can accomplish big things but your mother is more personal. She cries. She talks to people and connects with them. I see that in both of you boys. In the smile on your face."

I love hearing about my mother from people who remember her. It's hard for me to remember her after so much time, so it's almost like I get to see glimpses of her again when people talk about her.

A few days later I get to sit down with Alayu and try to understand the root of this movement in Ethiopia. If anybody is the lynch pin in what is happening, it is Alayu Kebede. His English is as good as any Ethiopian national I have met on this trip so we sit without a translator.

One of my main goals of this interview is to find an answer to a question that has been haunting me. It is a question that someone very dear to me (an atheist) had challenged me with. And it is a very good question. He had asked me about missions and why would we destroy beautiful, ancient cultures by bringing in a new religion and making people conform to it.

But first I start by asking Alayu for context.

Tell me about what you have been a part of here.

Thank you so much, my brother, for letting me speak

about what God is doing in my country and east Africa.

Our vision is to plant 10,000 churches in the Eastern African region in the next 10 years. Our plan is to plant churches region after region. We have used this strategy to plant churches in each region in this country and the countries around it like South Sudan and Uganda. Previously we planted almost 1,700 churches in a previous program in a region called Benishangul-Gumuz. This region is on the border of Sudan. God has helped us to bring 100,000 converts to the churches. For the last four years we were called to Oromia (the current region near Addis Ababa) and we have planted 1,000 churches, and have brought almost 200,000 people to Christ. So our vision is to go to these nine regions of Ethiopia and plant 1,000 churches in each region.

I figure this is as good a time as ever to introduce the question that has been bothering me.

Why bring a new religion into a place when it will potentially cause violence and may destroy the original culture?

We believe in the Bible, and it says the only religion that will save people is believing in Christ. We have seen it bringing new life to lives that were miserable, lives that were addicted to drugs. The gospel is bringing peace and stability for community. I can tell you, when you see the world we have many crimes, wars and those religions that have been around for millions of years are committing crimes. There is so much trouble, so much terrorism. We are taking the gospel to these villages and countries and it brings peace and stability. Other religions, we have seen, have not brought any peace. The gospel is bringing peace. We have actually seen in our country where people who were killing each other, when we brought the gospel they became peaceful. They have become good people who are helping others. It is bringing peace and stability.

Do you have any specific stories of this?

Yes. In the Geldu area the people were killing each other and the government was not able to handle the situation. We brought the gospel to this area and now this area is a peaceful and stable people and community.

What are the specific ways in which it is more stable? Interpersonal dynamic? Infrastructure?

We have brought water, electricity, and medical treatment. And we have seen the community love one another, interpersonally. There is more development now. When people are killing each other, there is no stability. When we bring the gospel the people can interact together. They can work together. They can think about developing their community together.

What about Christianity makes this happen?

Christianity makes things happen because it is a life that thinks about people. Not about being self-centered. Christianity is about others. Living for others. Working for others. Sacrificing yourself for others. I mean, you came here, sacrificing your comfort to sacrifice yourself for others.

How has it affected your life specifically?

My family expected me to graduate as a doctor. But

God called me at 12 years old to be a church planter. A missionary. I respected God's calling. I have worked for the last 32 years in the church-planting ministry. My life is impacted so much. There is hardship and so much sacrifice, but nothing is more important than church planting, missions, impacting others, and saving others for eternity.

Can you tell some examples of how Christian life has affected raising children, having land, running businesses, and other aspects of your life, other than church planting?

I have 10 siblings, and 5 children. I am the oldest and all of my siblings have become Christians because of my ministry. Their life has been changed and transformed and they are all leaders of communities and churches. Christianity has impacted my family; all my children and brothers and sisters are Christians. I'm impacting my other relatives and many of them are coming to know the Lord because of my ministry.

How has their quality of life changed?

You know life isn't about just one thing. It is aspects of different things. Quality of living-- when you are a Christian your mind is renewed. And when it is renewed you think bigger than locally. You think globally though you act locally. So most of my disciples, my brothers, because they are Christians are working globally. They work for Compassion International, or for denominations. And when I see my friends who are not Christians, they are still in their local village. Their life is not even changed. Life gets better when you love God.

Can you tell me more about how you became a Christian?

I was 12 years old when I became a Christian. An American missionary came to our village and preached the gospel and I was very interested in their songs and their children training. So I went every time to their tent where they were teaching. So I believed in Christ as my personal savior. And God spoke to me. And from that day on I was a church planter.

How did you know it was God's voice?

It wasn't until I started planting churches in South Sudan and Uganda that I realized the voice had been God's voice. It had said, "You will be a leader for black nations."

What is your relationship with your wife like?

He breathes in deeply.

I was sent as a missionary in 1996 by the Blair Foundation and she was also one of the church planters in that organization. We got married after 3 years. It's our 15th year together. You know it's difficult being a wife of someone who travels and goes to different places. But she has a heart for missions so she cares for our children and I just have a wonderful visionary support and help from my wife. And we are so grateful for being together in the ministry.

How much of your vision comes from, or is supported by her?

100% she supports and 100% we work together.

How often do you get to see each other?

We live together. But I go away for training for about a week or two each month. But we are privileged being together, you know.

What would you tell Americans who are having trouble believing the stories of miracles happening here? And even if they do believe it, how should they apply it?

I can say that the miracles we are seeing today are in the Bible. We are applying the Bible in our lives. We are not bringing anything that is not written in the Bible. So we just use the authority God has given us as sons and daughters of the Lord. Driving out demons. Healing the sick. And we believe that these miracles and signs are just something that draws people to Christ. We are not impressed with the miracles. We use these things to bring people to the Lord. He is confirming his word is true through these miracles.

What would you say about science's role in what God is doing?

Miracles aren't the main purpose. The main purpose is saving lives.

God uses miracles and signs to bring people into his kingdom. Miracles aren't the main purpose. The main purpose is saving lives. But the humanitarian activity like clean water and medical are also tools, like the wonders and signs, to bring people to you so you can preach the gospel. The signs and wonders are things that bring people to you. And then you explain and prove that the word of God is true.

So medical help and clean water are tools to draw people to you and then you can present the gospel.

What message do you want to give to Americans?

I believe that this world is becoming complicated, and globalization is bringing people together and making people think differently. People are after knowledge right now. They think if you have knowledge, money and God, that is enough. But life is beyond even that, bigger than that. Life is giving yourself to others so that you can impact other lives. It is just not living your own life. You should not be self-centered. Give what you have.

But my people are not after knowledge or wealth. They depend on God for everything . . . their faith in God is what brings the miracles.

I know American people are the most giving people for the gospel and humanitarian work. And I respect Americans for the value they give to missions. But they are after knowledge. They do not need the wonders and miracles. But my people are not after knowledge or wealth. They depend on God for everything. They depend on God for what they eat, what they drink, for everything in their life. Their faith in God is what brings the miracles.

Being dependent on God brings the miracles.

Faith brings the miracles.

If you feel you have everything and are efficient you don't need to have faith to do something. But African people don't have anything so they depend on God and God is providing what they need.

Is it possible to have faith when you have everything?

Sure. Because it is a matter of intimacy with God. The poverty in Africa brought the people to relationship with God. Whoever you are if you have an intimate relationship with God you can have faith and do any miracle.

You are an American, you prayed for a sick woman and she was healed. And because of her healing people came to know the Lord. The most important thing is that she brought other people to the Lord.

Why would I give away what I have to take on someone else's vision for me (God's vision for me)?

Remember the wealthy guy who Jesus asked to give away everything and follow him? He said many people will get everything in this world and will still lose their life.

The problem is when people say we will be happy when we have everything. If they test the life they have in Jesus they will see the happiness they had from wealth doesn't compare.

What would you tell those who feel some sort of calling to Africa?

If they come and serve the needy their lives will not be the same when they go home. Their life perspective will change. Some people don't know the situation here and when they see how people, human beings created by God, live differently, they may even say, "I have too much and I need to give away to the people who are really needy." And some of the Westerners throw so many things into the trash, things that could have been a benefit, which could change many lives for people here.

And for Christians who come here, their faith will grow. You have grown in faith because you have seen God has done some miracles. Now you can go home and pray for miracles.

Their world perspective even may change if they come here. I lived all my life in Africa, in Ethiopia. My perspective may change if I go to America. Your worldview changes, your faith grows and your life perspective changes.

From an American's perspective it might appear that these pastors are bullet proof and we Americans still have normal every-day challenges. Can you tell me about challenges you've had and how do you get through those struggles as a man of God?

Since we are working on human lives and bringing

from darkness to light, always the darkness and the devil fight us. The devil fights us for taking his territory in any way he can. The most challenging part of my life is when brothers persecute me. When Christians persecute Christians. When they become jealous and want to take advantage of what God is doing. And want to even kill you. Not just the Coptics or Catholics. Even evangelists do this. Our brothers even threaten us for what we are doing.

The other challenge is struggling with finances. We want to do more, but we have to stretch. If I had the money today I could send 10,000 missionaries in Africa. With 30,000,000 dollars you could cover the whole continent with missionaries. Ten countries with 1,000 missionaries in each country.

What impresses me is that Jesus did what he could do. He didn't heal everyone in the world. He didn't visit every village in the world. He did what he could do with his human limitations. So if I could do what I can do it will please God. And my friends in America, do what you can do to save people from darkness and hell.

I urge the world. It's not about just Africa. It's about reaching the unreached people groups in the world. It might be in Brazil. It might be in Africa. It might be in Asia. It might be North America. It might be anywhere in the world. We must give what we can give. We must do what we can do.

I think a lot of people think they are saved because they grew up in a Christian nation and go to church. What would you say to the people who think they are

already saved but aren't?

Salvation is a personal relationship, and intimacy with God. Your personal relationship can be demonstrated by prayer, reading his Word, serving in the church and helping others. The Bible says that the religion that is most pleasing to God is helping widows and orphans. If you claim that you are a Christian you have to pray and read the Word and give away what you have for orphans, widows and other activities. If you live your life and pass away, you don't have any story. If you share your life for others, you have a story in God's kingdom.

Can a person have all those symptoms and still not be saved?

Do you remember Cornelius in Acts[3]? He was praying and he was a giving man. He was a giver. While he was praying God said, 'your prayer is wonderful. I have seen what you've done- it is wonderful. But there is something remaining. Send for a person named Peter and he will tell you what you should do. He called Peter and Peter told him you have done all these things, but you have something you need to do to be saved. Accept Jesus as your personal savior.

Especially the young people think because they are acting out church they are saved, but they have not confessed that Jesus is their lord and savior. If they haven't, their activities will not serve them.

What does that look like in someone's heart? What

---

[3] Acts 10

does that mean for someone's life?

If you have received Jesus Christ as your personal savior, your behavior, perspective, character should change. For example when you say Jesus is your personal savior, it means the spirit of the Lord controls your life.

Your anger is removed. Your sin is removed. Your actions- you express the love you have received in Jesus' action. Most people claim they received Jesus but they don't reflect it in life. Their life still hurts others. Remember Jesus cursed down a tree because it did not bear fruit? If we are in Christ we are renewed. We are a new creation. We have a new life. We must reflect a new way of life.

Is there anything else you'd like to say?

Yes, my opinion to the whole world is we are in an especially urgent call to save lives. To protect our nation from the invasion of Muslims. America, a Christian nation, has allowed Muslims to come to their nation. And the Muslims are building mosques and schools and even given some government offices and their intention is to take the whole world to be Muslims. So we are in a very urgent call to protect the nations, especially the Christian nations from being taken over. We are not protecting ourselves. We are not even going to protect others. We are giving up our nations to threats and invasion. As the church planters and missionaries we have to go out to the Muslim nations. Especially the Christian nations should protect their nations from the threat of Muslims because that brings death for their nation, in terms of spiritual and physical death.

In what ways?

What is happening in America, because it's open to anyone, is bringing terrorism. America fights terrorism by going to any other nation, but they are bringing terrorism to their own nation. Freedom is good but we should have a limit to what we let come in. We need to be thinking of the future generations. We may not be able to be Christian after forty years. All the Asian and European countries, even the Corinthians and Ephesians, and Turkey, were all Christian. But throughout all these years they have been taken over by Muslims. We are trying to go back and reach those countries after 300 years. They used to be Christian nations but now they are 100% Muslim. It's giving an assignment to the generation to come by inviting Muslims into our nations today. So we must protect the nations and reach out to the Muslims with the gospel of Jesus Christ.

Complicated but reality.

When the Muslims came to Africa they came to North Africa and Ethiopia at the same time. But Ethiopia was dominated by the orthodox and they fought the Muslims from coming in. But the native religions in North Africa allowed Muslims to take over and now they are fully Muslim nations.

We have remnants now. 62% of Ethiopia is Christian, meaning Orthodox, Catholic, and Evangelical. But the other nations were taken over.

Why is Christianity better than Islam moving in?

The whole world is under pressure from the Muslim movement and hundreds of people are dying because of their bad action and belief. Millions of people are dying in Iraq, Syria, and in different parts of the world. And we can't see any terrorism action by Christians anywhere in the world. Christian nations like America, or others, we don't see any terrorism action by Christian nations. All the terrorism threats are from the Muslims. Can you witness any bombing throughout the world from Christians?

What about Gaza, etc.?

The biblical history about Israel is clear. Israel is in God's mind and the Muslims don't accept that truth. Also, Israelites are defending their homeland. And most of their homeland has been taken by the Muslims. They are fighting for that. And they weren't even able to be in their country for thousands of years, until 1968. They didn't even have a homeland. Even the temple is under the Muslim temple. So they are looking to get their own land back.

So it is not about freedom, actually. It's thinking about generations. We might declare freedom in any nation, but if that freedom brings the destruction of the generation to come, we have to be a leader that protects them. The Muslim strategy is not only preaching their Muslim religion, they are marrying Americans and Ethiopians. They have all kinds of strategy to invade a country. If you, especially as a Christian nation, allow them to settle in your nation. . . I mean if it happened for Ephesus, Thessalonica, Colossae, and Philippi, don't you think it will happen to America or Ethiopia?

I mean, do you think Americans will still send

missionaries after 20 years? Maybe not. It is declining because the perspective of the leaders of the nation has changed. 20-30 years ago the American government was supporting missionaries to go to the world. Now the only organizations sending missionaries are the church and now the government is weakening the church, not giving enough support for the church. So when the leadership perspective changes the nation can struggle.

So some of the ways Muslims invade nations are through marriage, violence, and business. In fact most investments (Foreign Direct Investments) in Ethiopia are from Turkey and Saudi Arabia. They are coming through investments and invading the nation. They come with two purposes. One, to get money, and two, to make it Islam.

Also, they invade by opening schools. I have an experience in this. An Arab Muslim opened a school in Addis Ababa and he asked all the girls to wear a veil. They weren't even Muslim!

Or they open a medical clinic in a Christian dominated area and bring them free treatment to bring the teachings. They do the same strategies as Christians.

Then what is the difference?

Ours is life. The gospel is life and their preaching is taking people to death. They pay whatever money to send their young generation to Arab countries to study, and learn Islam, and get masters and doctorates in Muslim and something else. Like a degree in social service maybe, or other things, but they teach people how to invade other nations with Islam. And because they have the education they get the position in the government. And with the position in the government they get access to land to build mosques.

In Uganda, their strategy is to have a mosque every ten miles.

I'm sorry to harp on this so much, but what is the difference between the life Christians say they bring versus the life Muslims would say they bring?

Everybody should agree life should be peaceful and joyful. And life should be living for others. But the Muslim position is they believe that if they kill you, a Christian, they go to heaven. As a human no one can allow or believe that killing someone can save anyone for eternity.

Just then my dad burst into our interview, put his hands on my shoulders and said that a woman was just healed of being blind. "Do you want to come over and see her, Alayu?"

Alayu excitedly exclaims, "Praise God!" And as I quickly ended the interview so we could go see, he says one last thing.

"So Christianity brings life."

And I responded. "And seeing is life."

We went over and investigated the healing. The blind woman had been to our medical clinic a few days prior and came back now being able to see partially. The doctors had given her tablets to take of Prednisone, which, among other things can reduce certain types of swelling. None of the doctors expected it to work but thought they should try, even if it was a long shot. And it appears that perhaps it took down some of the swelling behind her eyes. It appears that the hands of the

Christian doctors brought vision to a blind woman, maybe with a little help from God.

* * *

I think about what Alayu says and believes, why Christianity brings life and Islam brings death. But it is so hard for me, as well as other Americans, I think, to believe that any religion is bad and dangerous. We are trained to think all religions should be honored and accepted because that is one of the founding mantras of our nation: freedom and equality for all. But I see what Alayu is saying. If one of those religions is secretly bullying the rest through manipulation, and has a plan to eventually kill anyone they cannot convert, that should not be allowed! The peaceful religion should not be walked over simply because they will not resort to similarly violent measures.

And I don't think we can put all Muslims into one box. I assume that there is a difference between Muslims who move to America for opportunity and Muslim's who intend to take over.

But then I ask the question that is so prevalent in our culture. Why would God send people to hell because they got their religion wrong?

I remember that someone here told a story where Jesus had appeared to a group of Muslims in a mosque. Afterward everyone had said they saw Him. (After all I believe Jesus is considered a prophet in Islam.) And I've heard multiple times that Muslims are often having dreams in which they see Jesus too, calling them to follow him. So maybe there is one right religion, and Jesus himself is calling people from the other religions in very personal ways. I'm guessing that Muslims have their conversion stories as well. I would like to interview some Muslims when I get back.

I also think about how church planting happens in America. It is so often driven by the personality of the main pastor, and they do telecasts of that pastor to their church plants. But one of the other interviewers here mentioned it was interesting how the goal of these pastors was to start more churches, not make bigger churches. And they had no qualms about handing over a church to a new pastor. No pride in it. They just wanted more people to know Jesus.

Send off Celebration

Sending men off to die for the gospel

At the end of our week, we 27 Americans gather at the front of the warehouse-sized sanctuary, filled with the 272 Ethiopian missionaries that had gathered for the training.

We were about to go back to our lives of 9 to 5 and SUVs, but we were now standing in front of these men that will offer their lives to spread the gospel. Men who may never come back. Some of us are the monetary backing, and some of us are a little bit of medical help. But these men, the ones with a simple faith are about to go out into a world of people who want to kill them, curses that want to cut them down, traps waiting for them in the weeds, and governments that will work against them.

After addressing all of the missionaries with a few words Alayu turns to us Americans and says, "You are our family and we will serve in unity with you even until our deaths."

Then he tells the missionaries, "These Americans are taking your miracles, and the miracles that they have been a part of here back to America." He looks at me out of all of them and says, "Like Ross." And he looks at the rest of us, "And like the medical team." And then he tells us they will be praying for us. That these sentries of faith were praying for us.

> *"You are our family and we will serve in unity with you even until our deaths."*

Then Ray, the American leader asks us to get up and pray for them, similar to what we did at the church at the beginning of the week. So we each stand up, clumsily side-by-side, as they form lines in front of each of us. We are given an embroidered towel and a metal pin of praying hands to give to each of them to show we are with them in spirit. And we do our best, with our shallow faith, and distracted hearts, to pray for them and commission them to go sacrifice their lives for this faith we say we have.

We stand before these men. We who will go back to America, drink our beer, and chat about the game. We who will pop into coffee shops and chatter with our neighbors, silent about what Jesus has done for us because it might make someone uncomfortable. Or it might *not*, you know? And these men are trekking and preaching and praying and fasting and loving until their feet are raw, and voices hoarse so they can bring Jesus to the sick and weary who don't yet know about him.

Alayu then asks them to keep praying for us Americans. I lean back and whisper to the person next to me, "These men who are about to go and give their lives for the gospel are praying for us!"

And one of the other Americans who heard me leaned back and said, "It's okay. Don't feel bad about it. We each have our role."

Before the meeting is done Alayu announces there had been enough money raised to give 7,200 Bibles to them and their ministries. And he announces they were now sending their first missionaries to South Uganda.

But then Ray challenges us to keep praying for them when we go home. And he challenges us to challenge our churches to pray for them.

* * *

So I challenge you, my reader. If you have given me this moment with your eyes in this book, can I ask you to give this moment to them?

Let's think about those men walking through lands of opposition, seeking the sick to heal, and the possessed to set free, and the villages for which they would die to bring to Christ. Maybe we can try and understand their situation. And then let's pray with any desire we can muster, any desire the Holy Spirit can give us. Pray for Abdisa, and Girma, and Tesfaye, and the other Tesfaye, and Alayu. And the 250 or so others doing the same things as they. Place Ethiopian pastors on your prayer list. And then please pray for them.

It's so humbling to think we would be praying for these men. But like my friend said, "We each have our role." I guess we just do our best with what we've been given.

Jesus didn't heal the world in his life. He did what he could with the life he had. And that is what we can do. Every person you sit next to on the plane that may need to be heard, and who may need prayer. Each homeless person seeking shelter. The orphans and widows of your neighborhood, or whatever might be the modern day equivalents. Maybe that is the old woman who is barely able to take care of herself next door. Lets rake their yards or knock to say hi. Lets take our headphones out to smile and say hi and remember their names. And let us always be ready to pray for and with people.

I have heard these miracles and it appears I have even been part of one myself. And like Alayu said in front of them all, I bring it back to America with me. So hear my story. Believe. And help others do likewise.

Ray Noah

The history of Petros Network

(Video interviews:

part 1: http://bit.ly/1JvruVU

part 2: http://bit.ly/1JPlF7T)

I interview Ray in his and Linda's room. It is the last day of the trip and the bustle of organizing the remaining medical supplies is happening just outside the door. My dad offered to join me in this interview and now operates the video camera beside me.

My dad and I have gotten some great time on this trip to talk and work beside each other. He has shown me things here I've never seen before and told me stories about this place he has poured his life into. I have seen and heard from these people

the impact he has had on their lives, Ray being one of those.

I have gotten to see what my father does. And now he is joining me to help me and to see what I do. We are sitting side by side again, like on the airplane trip out here. We are sharing life together again like we have been for this whole trip, like not only father and son, but also like friends.

He is an excellent man, and has loved me well.

Ray has been one of his long time friends and, in fact, I found out that my dad was involved in the founding of the whole ministry, advising and pioneering new aspects of it from the beginning.

Ray is a tall, lean man, clean cut, with dark hair. He has an energetic, unassuming, easy-talking charisma. Good-natured jokes slip from his mouth easily like birds and he has moved on to the next subject by the time they land on the person. His face and hands are animated as he tells me his story and smiles break through when he tells the more entertaining parts. He chokes up when he talks about God's beautiful miracles in his life and losing his deep friend, Charles Blair.

Why do you care so much about this ministry?

I've always loved missions. I grew up in missions churches. Even as an adult. Linda and I have always had a heart for that.

The first time I came here though, that changed. I was in Asosa for ten days. I thought, "What in the world am I doing here?" It was an ugly, poor, dirty town. It was the last place I wanted to be. But over the course of ten days I realized God had dislocated my heart. And he had put a great love in my heart for Ethiopians and Africa. Everything began to converge. God began to pour into me the morals that now make up the Petros Network. I think God just literally reached down and put my heart on the other side of my chest. And I've been in love with planting churches every since.

Tell me about Charles Blair.

Well, Charles Blair was a well-known pastor. One of the premier pastors in America. He was like a pastor other pastors looked to for inspiration. My dad was a pastor and he talked about him. Charles pioneered a TV ministry in the Rocky Mountain region. He started a church of just a few people and he grew it to several thousand.

Well, when I was in Bible school Charles did a weeklong teaching on spiritual emphasis at my school. And I said to Linda, if I were to ever work in a church, I would want to work for Charles Blair.

Well, low and behold, after graduating, I worked in a church and after about 7 years, the pastor retired and I was ready to move on. And Charles Blair called me and asked me to be his executive pastor. So a dream I had back in college came true.

I remember back to when my family attended that church, Calvary Temple, for years when I was young. My brothers and I even went to the private school hosted in that building until I was in sixth grade. I remember Pastor Blair. And I remember Ray when he was a pastor there and I remember Linda and their daughters who were about our age and incredibly cute, always sitting in the front row.

I also remember how consistent it was. My mom and dad

took us to church every week. They paid for our private school. I realize this is another way my dad took good care of me when I was young. And now he is here beside me working the camera. He has loved me so consistently well for so long and it took a trip to Ethiopia to give me a glance down memory lane where I could be reminded of that again.

Ray continues.

I worked for him for 8 years. During that time he became my spiritual father, my pastoral mentor and just a close friend. Even after I left for Oregon, where we were from, we still stayed in touch. We were still on the phone once a week. Friendship. And then I left Portland and went to California to be a senior pastor there. It was then we got really connected. I brought him out to speak. He asked me to be on his foundation board; he was planting churches and no longer a pastor at that time. We just got a lot closer the older I got and the older he got.

Then Ray answers the question I was going to ask: "How did this lead to ministry in Ethiopia?"

So the Ethiopian connection was kind of a God thing for us. Some Ethiopian executives that worked at Compassion International in Colorado Springs asked to become part of our church, Calvary Temple in Denver. They met with us and told us, "We have 3,000 or 4,000 ex-pats in Denver and we need a church for them. Can we be part of your church?" We really liked them, and we had a tradition of hosting other ethnic churches, so we said, "Why not?"

So we decided to work together. But these guys were different. They didn't just want a room to rent. They really wanted to be a part of our fellowship. There were 75-100 of these ex-pats that really wanted to become members. They did baptism and stuff. They got their kids to be integrated in our Sunday school. They put on dinners for us. They put on their own services because they still spoke Amharic, but they became part of our DNA and we became part of theirs.

I suddenly remember seeing these strange dark people in colorful clothes walking through the halls when I was young. And how strange to think that it was those subtle clues in my past that foreshadowed, and played a part in me being in Ethiopia today.

So when the communist government here in Ethiopia fell, they started inviting Charles to come over and do leadership development because most of the pastors had been in prison, had been killed, had fled. So there was a real lack of spiritual leadership here.

That ultimately led to him finding sponsors for 300 of those. And in those original 300 there were a couple of key guys. Alayu and his wife Yegala, and Beckala. Those were three of the original church planters that went out under the Blair foundation.

So that kind of got started. Now fast-forward to 6 years later. I was now pastoring a church in the Bay area. Charles had retired from pastoring Calvary Temple but at age 84 he was still traveling to Ethiopia to do training.

God said, "I didn't ask you what you don't have. I asked you what you have."

Well he had been in Ethiopia and the president of one of the 9 federal regions, a far western, remote, primitive region was an evangelical Christian, the only one in the federal government. He was a fairly young guy. And he thought, "I need to use my position to further the gospel. I want to win my region to Jesus. And I think the way to do that is to plant churches. There are 3000 villages in my region. If someone could help me plant 1000 churches in 1000 villages, those churches would reach the other 2000 and my region would be won for Christ." He went from one organization to another looking for resources. But no one would help hm. Somehow he met with Blair and asked him to plant 1000 churches. Charles said, "YEAH!"

Ray's face lights up excitedly impersonating Charles.

So he gets on the plane and starts to think, "I'm retired. I'm 84. I don't have resources. What did I just agree to?"

So he started to hand-write a letter telling why he couldn't do it after all. But as he's writing down all these reasons why he couldn't do it God said to him, "Charles, I didn't ask you what you don't have. I asked you what you have." And Charles said, "Lord, all I got now is friends." And the Lord said, "Good. Tell your friends, and watch what I do."

So Charles flies home, gets off the plane and calls me up. I'll never forget the day. I'm sitting in my office in California and I get the call from Charles and we're talking and he's so excited. He's like a schoolgirl. He said, "Man, we're going to plant these 1000 churches in this region and here's the plan I'm thinking about, you know?" He's going on and on and on. And then he says, "So what do you think of that?" And I'm thinking, "Sheez, you're 84 years old. You oughta take a nap or something." But I thought, "He's so thrilled. This is just giving him energy so I said, "Man, that's a great idea. I think you oughta go for it."

And then he says, "Okay, so will you help me with it? I kind of felt trapped after I just encouraged him to go for it and I said, "Yeah. . . Yeah, I'll help ya."

We gathered 100 American pastors in Denver and we kind of laid out this plan. This is the region. This is the plan of how we're going to do it. This is what the cost per church is.

And we're going on and on and on building this thing up. And we did the same thing to them that he did to me. We asked, "Do you think this is a good idea?" And they all said, "Yeah! You should go for it." And then we said, "Well, will you help us?"

I think most of those 100 pastors committed to planting churches. I myself agreed to plant five of them. They were $1,850 a piece- to plant one, to support the pastor, buy Bibles, do training, that kind of stuff.

My church in California, well, we were already up to here in missions. *Ray holds his hand above his head.* I thought, 'It's gonna take about $10,000 to do 5. I'm not really sure we can do it,' but I just kind of felt like we needed to. So I went back to my church board and said, "Man, does this sound like a good idea?" They said yeah, and so I went to the church and said, "Just pray about this. I don't want you to give to it right now because you might be excited because I'm excited. Because if you give to this it's gotta be above your tithe, your offerings, above your missions tithe because if you rob Peter to pay Paul then I'm in trouble. So if God speaks to you, help sponsor these churches. If he doesn't speak to you, don't do it." So I made my church pray for it for a month.

Well during that month, knowing the commitment Sunday was coming, I'm starting to stress about everything; I know what people are going to do. They're going to take out of their tithe. They're going to take away from missions to pay for this and I'm going to have a problem. And so I'm just fretting about the money issue.

And God spoke to me, just this internal prompting I couldn't deny. He said, "Ray, if you will take care of the things I care about, lost people, I'll take care of the things you care about."

"Ray, if you take care of the things that I care about, lost people, I'll take care of the things you care about.

I said, "Okay. You got a deal, God."

Ray makes a hand shaking gesture and smiles at me.

So commitment Sunday comes and I'm thinking I'm probably the only one who really cares enough about this to do it so I don't know what's going to happen. I had faith that we would get five churches supported.

That day we raised enough money to plant 131 of those 1,000 churches. So I knew we were onto something that was of God at that point. And it dramatically changed my life and our church. That Sunday we became a missional church. And all the other issues and challenges became secondary. We were focused on changing the world.

An interesting thing happened. The month that we made those commitments, our tithe jumped 30%. That's unheard of. You might jump 10% in a year but we jumped 30%. The Lord said, "If you take care of the things I care about I'll take care of the things you care about." And he was just proving to me that's the way he operates.

Our missions giving increased 200% that year and 100% the next year, on top of the Ethiopian giving. Every year we were growing, growing, growing in our missions giving.

This just showed us the word of the Lord is true. The more we give away, the more he gives us to give away. It's this cycle of generosity. This cycle of blessing that we came into. That reshaped the way I think about church and missions and walking in faith with God.

Well, fast-forward a few years when I am coming back to work in the old church I had been a part of in Portland. Their senior pastor had left and they wanted us to come back. They had been recruiting us for a year. We didn't think we'd leave California, but at the end of the day we felt like God told us to go back. But I told them, "But, guys I have this church planting thing in Ethiopia. This comes with us."

By this time Charles Blair was sick and I was sort of running the organization. And the church in Portland said, "Yeah, we know about that. We've been watching that and we want to have that too."

So we come back and after about a year I know it's about time to start planting some more churches. So this time I have a little more faith. Last time I had faith for five and we got 131. Let's do 250 and that's going to be a real stretch.

And it was the same situation with our budget already being tight. But now I knew what God had already promised me: "If you take care of the things I care about, I will take care of the things you care about."

So I took it to my board and made them pray about it for a month. I said, "I know you guys have seen what we've done, and you believe in this and you believe in me and I think you'll say yes. But don't tell me yes until you pray for it. Because if God's not into it, we don't want to do it."

They came back and told me, "Yes, but not just *do* this. We need to do it unapologetically, with 1000% of our effort." So I took it to the congregation and asked them to pray for a month too. Again this commitment would have to be above and beyond what they are already giving. So commitment Sunday comes, and I'm up there again wondering, what if no one gives? So it's kind of that moment of doubt again.

They begin to walk their commitments down.

Ray gets choked up and pauses.

That Sunday we gave enough to plant 364 churches. And again I'm thinking, "God, you are faithful to your promises. Your word is true."

And that really launched us into orbit. As a result of

that our church has been blessed in lots of things.

Our finances have been blessed. We gave $1.7 million last year for missions. And as a result of all this growth, other churches want to be a part of it.

And at that point Linda and I realized we needed to make a church-planting organization so that other churches can give to something that will plant churches. So, three years ago we launched the Petros Network to do that.

In those last four years the growth in Ethiopia has been spectacular. And even in South Sudan we have 100 churches. We've planted churches in Uganda. We're looking at maybe Brazil soon.

In four years we have grown to 1100 churches, 200,000 converts. And these are not inflated numbers. Part of our deal is real accountability, transparency. We literally have 200,000 people converted out of darkness. Previously unreached people.

It's a movement. It's not a program. It's not a paradigm. I think God has used our organization to create a church-planting movement.

I want to get an idea of how much of his life he has sacrificed to pursue this mission, but I think he's too humble to tell me directly.

Now I'll ask a back door question, because I don't think you'd answer the front door version. What has your *wife* given up for this ministry?

100% of what we have raised in the Petros Network goes to where we said it would go. We don't take a salary. We haven't hired staff. Literally it goes to these church planters.

So, I have really stretched my staff. My church staff has done this with me as volunteers. Extra credit. And at the top of that heap is my wife Linda. Just a brilliant person. A great organizational mind that has really come along side me to put the structure and process to the Petros Network. I get to focus on the vision and training, but she has to do the million and one other things to make it sustainable and reproducible.

So, she works late into the night many days. She's a pastor in our church, running communications, spiritual formation, and discipleship in a sizable church. And on top of all of that she's taken on the role of vice president of our organization and really chief operations officer. So it has come as probably more of a sacrifice to her than even to me.

She's just as passionate about it as me. Beyond church planting she's taken on what we call redemptive lift. Part of that is to form a widows empowerment program and she's really passionate about that and it has come at a great cost to her.

But now I realize I can't stretch my people much further. We're at a point where we need to grow our organization in a whole new way.

You know, I'm a guy always in a throws of a new vision. They hear me coming down the hall saying, "I have this idea." And they're like, "Oh great what are we going to do now?"

There was a great missionary to China in the 1800's, named Hudson Taylor. As he was dying they asked him about what he did and he said, "It was no sacrifice."

Ray chokes up as he tries to say the next line. Tears well up in his eyes.

It was no sacrifice. And . . . I'd give my life for this. I think Linda would too. Your dad would do. We would lay down our lives for these people, because they are the ones that are really sacrificing.

If people want to pour into this, what do you need? How can they help?

We've got a great thing going on here. I never want to reduce The Spirit to a formula, because He's not. But we know how to plant churches. I say it in humility because we just stumbled into this. But we know that for $2,100 for this area of the world, we can plant a church. $2950 to plant a church in South Sudan.

You give us your missions resources and we'll change the world. One church will quickly have 100's of converts. If we plant 1,000 churches in a region, that region will surrender to Jesus Christ. I've come to believe through this that we can change the world. If I have $300,000 I can plant 100 churches. If I have $3,000,000, I could plant 1000. The equation just goes up.

If you want to make the best investment of your life you will see so much reward. There will be souls standing in eternity some day because of the investment you made. I've experienced that and believe it. Money equals souls. I mean Jesus said that in one of his parables, "Buy for yourself friends in this world so that they will welcome you into the eternal kingdom.[4]" I'm convinced he's talking about missional investment. Because we know in missions around the world it's a resource challenge. Agencies need resources and so do we. And we have a track record to prove that.

Of course we need prayer. We need expertise coming. We need doctors coming. Builders coming. But we need resources because we can translate those resources into eternal souls.

Can you speak to our role as Americans?

Teams that come over hear the stories of miracles, healings, people being raised from dead and they say, "Why can't we have this in America?" It can happen over there but this is the gift of the Ethiopians and others we're working with over here. They have simple faith and they see these kinds of things. They weren't doing this before we came. We don't have in America what they have in Ethiopia, but they don't have what we have either. So it's been this amazing congruence, this amazing confluence of their simple faith and our resources, and our ability to train and organize. And together this spiritual explosion is happening here. So I try not to feel bad about the gifts we don't have, that they have. Or the gifts we have that they don't have. This is how the body works together. Together we leverage our gifts.

---

[4] Luke 16:9

Tell me about disciple making.

I've realized this is a baton passing. I am not going to fumble the baton. I want to unleash something in my people, like Blair unleashed in me. They'll do something somewhere, I know they will. You can't walk away from something like this unchanged.

So I let them see the organization. I drill into them the values. It's funny to catch them in their unguarded moments, sort of spewing back what I've said to them. And then I know okay, yeah, they're getting it. That's a big part of what drives me these days. We've spelled things out so that my disciples are getting the ideology.

And I do that with my church. I may only have 15 years left! What a waste of kingdom resources it would be to have to reinvent everything. What a waste not to hand it all over and pass it on. You should be able to take it and run with it to the next level.

My dad next to me asks Ray the next question.

Is it fair to say Africa is primarily a country of relationships?

I think the name Petros Network is prophetic. We realized we had no idea how to do so many of the things we wanted to do. So we had to build a network of like-minded partners who have the same value but different expertise.

During the first go around with Blair, I knew we couldn't do it all. We didn't know how to build hospitals or write micro-grants. So that's how the word 'network' came up. We wanted to bring in Kingdom partners. We work with 30 different Ethiopian denominations.

And a big part of making a network work is unity. That's why it's one of our values. Collaboration is a value. We stumbled upon it but we found out, as much as anything, God blesses unity. It says in the Bible, when brothers combine in unity, God commands blessings. He commands it[5].

I think he likes to see his kids playing together in the sand box. He says, "I like that! I'm going to bless that."

And it says in the Bible, "It takes every effort to keep unity in the Spirit." So we have to give every effort to it.

But it's worth it because that's what God blesses.

I jump in again to ask the next question.

Okay, one to look inside now. To get to know your heart more. If God asked you to give up one thing for Him, what would be the hardest thing?

Interestingly I was thinking about that 2 or 3 days ago, in the wee hours here when you can't sleep, for whatever reason I had been contemplating God's offer to Solomon. He said, "Ask anything and I'll give it to you."

He doesn't ask for wealth or fame or power. He said, "God, I just want wisdom."

[5] Psalm 133:1-3

So I thought, *God, if I could ask You for anything what would it be?*

So I was thinking about these things. I want my family to all be in the kingdom some day. I want my church to be blessed. I want this African mission to grow beyond our wildest expectation. And I don't want fame or money because I see how it corrupts. I want Jesus to be famous.

So I was thinking about all these things. But then it struck me. You know what I want more than anything else?

> *One day we'll stand before God and he'll ask us, "What did you do with what I gave you?"*

I just want to be found faithful. I want Him to say, "Good job. Well done. Enter into my joy." I would be willing to give all of this up, if he asked me to, just to be called faithful by him.

Because one day we'll all stand before God and he'll ask us, what did you do with what I gave you?

And I want him just to say, "Son, Well done. I'm proud of you. You did what I asked."

So I'd give up everything, Ross. And it would be hard. Giving up my church would be hard. Giving up my health would be hard.

But if I could do that and sacrifice to do what he asked me to do, I'd do it in a heartbeat.

* * *

Giving up family and others for the sake of God seems
a counter-American idea. We have often made the
ultimate morality be 'take care of others.' But I think it
really does come down to this: that our will does not
know best. God's will knows best and the ultimate trust
would be to do what you think seems uncaring if he
were to ask for us to. And if we trust him to be faithful
and loving, we believe that in the end his will is for the
most health and beauty for the most of his creations.

The Ethiopian missionaries told about healing miracles,
usually stemming from people being freed from
controlling forces in the spiritual realm. That is a realm
they are used to and deal with every day.

But Ray talks about miracles happening in America in
the financial realm. Could it be that this is a lesson in
being freed from slavery to America's main, controlling
god? Money? And just like in Ethiopia maybe we can
be freed from what most controls us by letting God
come in and replace our attachment to it with himself.

Linda Noah

Widows and orphans

(Video interview:

Part 1: http://bit.ly/1NF6lue

Part 2: http://bit.ly/1Lw1yfc)

I get to interview Ray's wife, Linda in the same room shortly after he and I are done. She is a slightly quieter presence that moves around making sure things are running smoothly. She is confident, stylish and sharp. And when she sees a child in need, or talks about the difficult things they've been through, or sees God coming through in beautiful ways, she keeps her strong composure and wipes tender tears away.

Linda, I know you're involved in helping widows and

orphans. Can you tell me where that comes from?

What we're doing is based on a scripture. When John the Baptist sent his guys over to see if Jesus is the Messiah Jesus responds, "Go tell John what you see."[6]

It's just this whole idea that Jesus did things in word *and* deed. So we've decided that there needs to be a balance of those two: church planting balanced with helping in practical ways, which we call redemptive lift.

We push the church planting because it's easier for people to want to give to medical or dental. We've tried to balance the finances, 60% to church planting and 40% to redemptive life.

When we originally planted churches, $150 would go to help them create sustainable businesses that would support the church. The money went to the church, not the church planter, in case he moved on, and the church would get to keep the livestock bought with the business money. But what we found is that the churches became self-sustainable from raising the livestock and from the tithe. And it really became like the New Testament church, bringing what they had together to support the church.

Some planters will make a church sustainable, raise another leader, and go on to plant another church. Some of them follow us from region to region. One guy planted 41 churches in the old region. And he moved to this region with us, but before we had even gotten here

---

[6] Matthew 11:1-6

he had arrived and launched his church. So they're machines. They're warriors.

We're also trying to train them up on how to lead. Petros sends church planters, but trains them to develop the indigenous leaders on their own with the ultimate goal being the indigenous leader will take over. We lift Alayu up because he is the indigenous leader.

And then there is the redemptive lift aspect. Most of these people live on $1.25 per day, which puts them in extreme poverty. So we develop the indigenous leader by teaching him to make the town better. Most of the time these villages have a witchdoctor in charge. He has the most knowledge and he leads the village. So then our church planter comes into the village and there is a spiritual confrontation. And we have lots of stories of the witch doctor falling over dead, or their houses getting struck by lightning and stuff.

Then our person is the leader. And we have trained them how to bring in things like sanitation, marriage and family instruction like how to honor your wife, and how to care for your children.

We had a story of a man who met the pastor and was standing there with his five wives. We have to engage their culture, and the pastor couldn't just tell him to send his other four wives away, because they would starve. So he instructed him, 'love your wives.' We have to be ready to modify.

Also, we would come in and love on their children, and teach the people the value of children's ministry. And now they will coddle their children and hold them whereas before they wouldn't at all. They used to hit them with switches and whips. Women and children have been treated like dogs. They have been the low caste in society, and then we come in.

So if you look at it, when we plant a church, there is proclamation of the word, but all of life should change.

We also try to bring in agriculture. We have a model farm out back. *She points to the back of their property.* So we can teach them. When we started they would just scatter the seeds. But we are teaching them to till it and plant it into rows, and we make sure they are pulling the weeds. Something that simple changes their harvest.

We also participate in a 50-acre farm that is about two hours from here. There we harvest teff, are raising beehives, goats, and oxen. For that we've put in an investment of funds and we try to hire widows and those less fortunate. That is so that in the event where we can no longer come or wire in funds they would be sustaining themselves.

We also have brought clean water. We have laid a mile of pipe and now are just waiting on a new pump so we can take water from a well and release it to a whole new region of Gojo. Most of the illnesses we are seeing right now are water born illnesses so this should help us solve that. We've also made a few wells in some of the remote villages.

Medical and dental clinics. In one region we brought in medical teams and medicines. We partnered with a hospital there that could only serve one million people. All their shelves were empty. We brought nine duffle bags of medications and medicines. It was such a big event the news media came out.

And now here, like you've seen, a group of medical professionals from Southeast Christian Church, and Parker Evangelical Presbyterian Church in Parker, Colorado have come out for a weeklong clinic for the locals.

It's been interesting. We had a list of different ways in which we wanted to provide redemptive lift, everything from widows and orphans, to clean water, to agriculture, to sports, to medical. And without knowing it each church that wants to be involved has chosen a different one of those areas. Not a single one of our partners from America, Canada, or Bermuda asked to champion the same area.

I'm always watching what works and what doesn't because once we get this established in Gojo we want to launch it into 1000 villages.

One dynamic that became a big one to me... you saw the extreme poverty. We didn't want to just give money away-- we don't want Americans to be seen in that way-- we've been careful to put the money through the church models and to always hire people to do things for us. Not just give money away.

Also, something I noticed very quickly was that women were doing all the labor; they were treated as low citizens. If you go out here you will see women carrying piles of sticks on their backs weighing 50-75 pounds. And they were the ones lugging the water and the wood to build the homes. They were caring for the children and doing all the cooking. And the men were just sitting around town, and in many cases getting drunk.

I noticed the children getting disrespected too and this upset me. I asked the Ethiopians who are the most desperate? Who is considered the lowest rung? And they told me it was probably the widows. And then also the orphans, because there are just so many.

And again we didn't want to pass out money so we collected 12 widows around us and began interviewing them. The majority of them were earning maybe 2 US dollars per week. So that would be about 8-11 dollars per month. But to give you an example, in the marketplace out here a skirt is 15$. So they were wearing tattered clothing. They were wearing clothes with holes in it, and layering all these different things just trying to even keep warm. And that's even less than the world poverty index of $1.25 per day. So I thought, what can we do to begin to shift this?

So we began by just getting to know them. We interviewed them. We found out how do they cook in their homes, how many meals, what are they eating, do they have latrines. 70% don't even have a bathroom hole attached to their homes. They did it all over in the fields. And in one case we found they were going poop and pee where they were planting onions. So you can imagine the sickness that was spreading.

When we first went to one of the widows' homes I was devastated. Our people told me, "We can't sponsor her because she's too rich." She had mud floors. Mud walls. She might have had a few dishes in her house, like little china cups, and some Tupperware things they were using as dinner plates. There were 5 people in a bed.

There was newspaper taped on the wall to keep the wind from rattling things to death.

Just then, in our interview one of the American doctors knocks and brings in "Widows and orphans stuff: a box of pre-natal things." She points where to put them and says, "Beautiful. Anything you want to bring in!" And she continues the interview.

So my Ethiopian helpers responded, "Did you not see she had a bag of coal? And she had two chickens? She's too rich."

I began sobbing and I couldn't even lift myself off of the floor. The next morning we were going out again and I said, "I can't even visit these women if I have to make these decisions about the grants we are going to give them. I can't see them because I'll just give it all away."

So one day one of our Americans that had gone out to the widow's homes came to me and said, "I have a beef with you." And he started sobbing right there, a grown man. Then a woman followed him and was sobbing too. They said, "We have to be able to support these women."

This is our belief; you can't give money without education

So now for each widow we have her fill out a business plan and write down exactly what each expense would cost. And then we pull together her pastor, the widow, the translator and us, and fight with each other to determine how much this widow should get.

One time we found out one of the girls didn't qualify for the grant because she had a college education and had declined a job. So we thought she must not be so desperate. But her pastor came in and FOUGHT for her. It turned out she had declined a job because she would have had to move away and she wouldn't be able to support her family. We decided to give that widow a loan solely on the pastor's word. That widow today owns a seed and spice shop, a restaurant, and is launching a hotel. Unbelievable!

Pride and joy spreads across Linda's face.

We went and visited the hotel yesterday. It's gorgeous.

So, we do training with them. We teach them hygiene, cleanliness, women's hygiene. This is our belief; you can't give money without education, because money will go away, but education is a gift that never goes away. This next trip we have already sponsored another 6 women.

And to add onto that, we've launched this thing called the Tesfa project. We found that some of the widows couldn't uphold a business but they could work. So we are starting a business that people can work in. Right now we are partnered with a company to help sew school uniforms. In our center will be women's and children's clinics, a home management training area where they will learn how to cook and change some lifestyle things (sanitation is a big part of that), and then we're going to have a small daycare so as the women work we can help take care of the children. This way we can get them off the streets. What we've found with the widows is that the children can't go to school because they have to be out on the streets to get water and wood. We're trying to get them into school and get the widows into a trade so they can try to sustain a lifestyle. We're looking to build this pretty significant center next year.

How far do American dollars go for construction here?

I don't know if you've seen the school yet but we've invested $175,000. It's a big school and houses 286 students. The church was $75,000 just for construction. This guesthouse we're in is easily $75,000. We're about to add on a dining hall and training area where we can do smaller trainings and actually do a restaurant in this. And so who is staying in this place? Different teams stay here, even Olympians come and stay and train here. It's sort of the nicest spot in town. The goal behind that was to create income that would generate so that if we got called out of the country it would sustain itself. That is the plan. Sustainable. Sustainable. Sustainable.

What else would you like to tell Americans?

Something I would add to Ray's thing. We need funding like he says, but we need talent.

Redemptive lift has taken people who have brilliant minds and skills, not as theologians or pastors but in agriculture of engineering, water management, architecture, to use their skills for the glory of God.

We just started Petros Canada and someone up there said, "You must have some brilliant minds behind you." I thought, yeah we do. *Linda smiles.* And they're all volunteers. It's just people using how God has built them, and their passions for the glory of God.

We're going to sponsor a race, which a lot of the Olympic runners come to. They expect 40,000 people to show up. And we're planning to send out the church planters into it to evangelize to the people.

We use every vehicle under the sun to advance the kingdom.

She stops and thinks.

You know what I would want people to know? God created each of us unique with different passions and skill all for the glory of God. So it's not all about making an income or providing for our families. That's part of it but God created you with that mindset, and gift set to be used for His glory.

We have to earn a living but we need to use our skills unfettered, unselfishly for the glory of God. I think that makes God smile.

So for me, I ask why in the world did I run a company, and travel so much in my past. It was because God was preparing me for such a time as this.

Ray and I are a unique couple. He is the vision-caster; I just work on the systems, system, systems all around him. God put us together. We are like one head. I can almost hear what he's thinking and I start running to structure it. But you know, I need greater minds than me to go to the next level.

Is there anything else you'd like to talk about

regarding the widows and the orphans?

She sighs and speaks quietly.

Oh, I don't know. Come back in a year from now and you're going to be blown away.

You know, one gal this week, the doctors examined her and said within three moths she will be dead. She had five children and was severely malnourished. She could hardly hold her head up. We just took a photograph of her before she left. Well, later we took that photograph of her into town and asked people if they knew her. We found her and we agreed to send her 900 birr ($45) per month until we come back again in a few months so we can evaluate her for a job. And I gave her some clothes.

Linda smiles and points outside.

She just showed up here a few minutes ago. She was jumping and skipping and absolutely giddy. She wanted us to see how pretty she was in her clothing. There was a smile on every side of her face. I wanted her to see the doctor that had helped her. And when she saw him she ran up to him and wrapped her arms around his waist, shaking, shaking, shaking. He has not only transformed her by connecting us to her, but her five children also forever.

It's not about the money; it was about the talent of that doctor. It's about the talent of my team. Yes, these people did give up money and vacation time to get here, but bringing the skill set over here is a bigger gift than the money.

The pastors are proud of what they have done with the

money we have given them. We give it to them with an expectation but we want it to be done in their way. We have tried to train some of them in some things like construction, plumbing, grout, and electrical. For example, I had never seen a toilet here in Gojo before we got here and trained them. When they make something it is low quality, it leaks, and it's not perfect but it is theirs, and they are proud of what they have done. The first time we were teaching them painting we painted a hospital room. Then we gave them the paint for the outside walls and when we came back they were also painting the rocks. We teach them but we want them to do it in their own way.

But regarding the money, even with the church planters it is not about the money. They are not getting money equitable to their sacrifice. The money has helped the church planters sustain their lifestyle and the money has truly escalated the spread the gospel, but I think they'd do it anyway. We've just enabled a bigger army. What we've done would have taken 40 years to do without our money.

We need money but it's not about the money. It's about people who are compelled by the call of God to see something bigger than themselves. To give themselves to something bigger than themselves.

* * *

Throughout this interview I couldn't stop thinking of the person who is very dear to me, the atheist, who had asked that haunting question, "Why would we destroy a beautiful, ancient culture by bringing in a new religion and making people conform to it?" I think Linda's stories of how Christianity is teaching the culture not to treat the women and children as animals, and training people to farm better and run businesses better and develop sustainable comfort has given me an answer.

Add to that the stories about Christianity releasing people from demons that were making them sick, lame, insane, and even making them want to kill others, and I think I finally believe that Christianity is the answer.

That week the medical team saw 830 patients plus 100 dental patients.

Conclusion
To believe or not to believe

I think the natural skeptic in us Americans searches for the faults in these stories as excuses not to believe them. There are definitely a lot of details in these pages that seem contrary to the model of the world many of us have set up in our minds and that's why it's hard to believe.

But I think that for most of us who choose not to believe these stories, it will not be because they don't stand up to scrutiny. It will be because we don't want to change the way we think. We'd have to figure out how everything else we've concluded can fit into this new view of how the world works. And then we might have to change the way we do things.

For me, I've been asking myself difficult questions, looking for answers that will explain the inconsistencies in the world and in my faith, since I was young. And I have held up different models of reality in my head to see which one most accurately matches how the world works. None of the models have fit perfectly, but after adjusting it to accommodate things I've learned in Ethiopia, it's filled in some holes and gotten closer than anything else I've found. See the following section, "My Updated Model of Belief," for my model and how it has been adjusted by what I have heard on this trip.

For most of us who choose to believe these stories, I think it will be because we first think they are actually plausible, and then because we *want* the world to be that type of world. We will want it enough that we will let it change the way we think.

Only you can decide. There is no scientific evidence proving that the spiritual world doesn't exist, but as shown in these stories there is much experiential evidence saying that it does. So, because it is plausible, this means the choice of belief is in our hands. It is a gift we have held in our hands since birth.

There is no scientific evidence the spiritual world doesn't exist, but as shown in these stories there is plenty of experiential evidence saying that it does.

And the fact that this possible reality implies there is a powerful king of a coming kingdom who is delighted to forgive our wrongs and is fighting for our good makes it an attractive option to me.

And then if we choose to believe, the challenge that we are to approach for the rest of our lives becomes to figure out what it means to be willing to live and die for this king who lived and died to have a relationship with us.

My Updated Model of Belief

How Ethiopia solved the tough questions of my culture

Here are my answers to some of the hard questions of our time, some of them being informed by what I've experienced in Ethiopia.

How could God exist and still allow so much suffering?

Girma Dorsisa stated that God lets suffering happen because it brings people back to himself. I think that is a great explanation for a lot of cases.

Also I have started asking the people I know who have suffered most if they would take back the suffering if they could, and so far, the ones who have made it out of the other side have thought hard and then said no; they would not give up the suffering. And they said they wouldn't because it was the suffering that had drawn them to know God as deeply as they do.

I know there are horrible stories that end in only despair and isolation. And I don't know how God can look at that and not move. But maybe He has, in a way. And maybe He hasn't, but we just don't know. I think we can only decide for ourselves, and what God has done in our lives. We don't know what suffering has done to people, or why God allows it, but in the end we only have our own experience with it.

And if this is any consolation, I think the most pain that can be felt in the world is only as much as one person can feel in one moment. A pain worse than that cannot be felt, except maybe if you are God, who feels the pain of all of His children together. And even pain for an entire life is small in comparison to eternity.

The Christian model says pain exists because God thought it important to give us the freedom to choose, and we chose to do things our own way, and our own way brought lots of pain with it. And even today we believe that the world has been given over to the control of selfish beings. God steps into the world from time to time, even though it has become like enemy territory to him, and he still touches us in ways that will help us see glimpses of him in the world he has allowed to choose its own way.

But I know that a lot of pain is horrible, and I feel the injustice in it. If I were God I don't think I would have given pain to the world if it didn't bring some sort of redemption with it. I know God is bigger than me, and enough of what I've seen shows that he is a loving God, so I will trust that he knows what He's doing with the parts of pain that I still don't understand.

Why would God create hell?

This is just my thought, but maybe he didn't create hell in the way Christians have traditionally pictured it, as an eternally punishment for a short lifetime of sin. But maybe he created heaven as a kingdom where He would be king and live with the people that wanted to live with Him, and do kingdom like He wanted to do kingdom. But maybe he made another place for anybody who wanted to do kingdom their own way, away from Him. And how we live our life reveals our answer to that question: do we trust *ourselves* with our life's decisions, or do we trust *Him* with them?

And since all the beings that lived in the place apart from God were the types that wanted to do things their own way, it would make for a lot of fights and oppression in that place. It would probably look like what we think of as hell.

I've seen on this trip how spirits can control humans for their own gain or pleasure. So if these same spiritual beings are in that place where everyone does what they want I'm guessing they could still control us there. And perhaps there are beings there that are even more powerful and have stewed on jealousy and injustice for centuries. Those beings probably make that place live up to all the connotations of the word hell, even though it was a simple choice of do we want to live in a kingdom run by God, or run by selfish beings like ourselves.

Why ruin beautiful indigenous cultures with our religion?

This one really bothered me until this trip. Now I see how the Christian ethic, when done correctly, has brought big improvements to these indigenous cultures. Women and children are actually treated as people, people become less selfish, and they try to make not only their towns better but also the world.

Spirits or just forces

The reason I think spirits are more than just forces, and have intelligence, personalities and wills is because Science hasn't been able to nail them down with experiments. Science only proves things that are reproducible. And beings that can think, react and choose don't always do the thing we expect of them.

Other religions

I now think Jesus is the true incarnation of God on this earth, as suggested by His dominance over other spirits in the Ethiopian stories.

However, it seems many religions are very similar to Christianity in ritual, story and morality, and therefore their techniques often satisfy our spiritual hunger. But ultimately if Jesus isn't in it, it seems like it is just a replica and just a salve on this life.

And when supernatural things happen in other religions it could be due to other spirits interacting with people in the world, posing as God or his servants.

But, I wonder if Jesus is visiting people within their separate religions. Upon an Internet search to see if the appearance of Jesus to Muslims was common, it appears Jesus has been busy.

Pastor Frank Costenbader, founder of Manifold Hope Ministries, publisher of the Isa Dreams website stated, "Nobody can get perfect statistics, but based on all our research, we believe that well over 1 million Jesus dreams and visions have occurred since the year 2000. This may be only 200 dreams each night among 1.6

billion Muslims worldwide." And there were sightings of Jesus within other religions as well. (Read more at www.wnd.com/2014/11/rising-number-of-muslims-reporting-dreams-about-jesus)

But even so, I would like to think that good-meaning people of other religions who never had dreams of Jesus, and who didn't hear a version of the gospel convincing enough to believe, will still be in heaven. I mean, maybe some do trust in His voice inside of them, even if they don't know it is Him. I hope that anyone who chooses to trust their life in the one who they think is God will be saved.

But ultimately if God chooses to condemn some, it is His prerogative. He created us. And his ways are greater than mine.

Why don't we see spirits in America?

Maybe they are purposely hiding because they know if we don't believe in a spiritual world, we won't believe in God either. And science has come up with reasons that make it feasible not to believe in God in the developed, enlightened world.

Christianity done poorly

I'm sorry. I hope I have shown here that even though God works through people, it doesn't suddenly make Christians infallible. And even when we think we are doing the right thing we may not be listening to the right voice. Or we have not waited to hear from God. There are a lot of ways to mess it up, but at least I think we are called to try.

For more of my thoughts on these subjects, visit my blog at www.RawSpoon.com and type your topic in the search bar.

Um, so what is this gospel thing?

How Jesus saves

A friend pointed out that a lot of Americans have never heard what this gospel is that is changing people's lives across the world. Well, "gospel" is an old word that means "good news."

And I think it is very good news. The first person to start telling this news was John the Baptist, who was Jesus' cousin. Before Jesus was famous, John was instructed by God to start telling people that we could apologize to God for our sins and trust our life with Him and God would forgive us and welcome us into heaven.

It had to work like this because although God is a god of perfect justice that thinks it's important for every wrong to be punished fairly, He also doesn't want us to be punished all the time and separated from Him (which would have to happen because we're so often sinning). So He went looking for a way that he could be both fair *and* loving. And he cleverly figured out a way to pay the price of our sin. He came down into a human body (Jesus) and said, "I'm God. I'll forgive your sins! Just trust your life with me!" And we humans executed Him because He threatened our authority.

But He let us.

In the end we made *him* pay for *our* sins. We trusted

our life with ourselves instead of with him. We wanted to be God instead of letting God be God and we committed the ultimate sin- we killed God for trying to take that position from us.

But he brought himself back to life, proving he was very much more God than we were.

And this is how he is so cool. So then he really had every right to say screw you guys for what you did to me, but He still found it in His heart to forgive every single one of us for every sin for all of time, if we will only repent and trust our life with him.

And this repentence can be done any time, anywhere, because it corresponds with a change in our hearts. But, we must weigh the cost. Are we willing to give up our plans and dreams for our lives if God were to ask them of us, and trust them in His hands instead of our own?

You can totally talk it through with God, and when you really mean it, you can just tell Him, in your head, or out loud, "I'm sorry for sinning against you and others. Please forgive me. I want to follow Your will from now on but I'm going to need your help. So please come into me and let's do this together."

There are like a billion people in the world that would rejoice if they found out you just prayed that prayer. So find one of us and tell us so we can party with you!

I would love it if you emailed me because you prayed that. It would be one of the most special moments of my life knowing that because of this book I will now have a new brother or sister in heaven.

Appendix on Transcription

For the interviews I have tried not to stretch the stories in any way but instead to do my best to report their meaning most readably and most accurately. At times I have changed the translations to make the sentences flow more smoothly and be clearer to the meaning. For example the translator left out a lot of articles (like a, an, and the) but I have often added them so that it would not distract from what I understood the meaning to be. And at other times I have left the translated sentence structure and word choice as is when I thought it better to hear the voice of the speaker and the translator.

There were times when I assumed certain things about some of the stories, and I added phrases when they were needed to clarify the meaning. Sometimes sentences were repeated in the interview to clarify the translation, but I chose to write the correct sentence only once.

Sometimes when an answer is disjointed, whether by disorganized thoughts or fumbling through translation, I've reorganized it to avoid distraction and still deliver most accurately what I understood the essence of the meaning to be.

I removed parts of the story seventeen times. But so that it doesn't seem like I am hiding something to manipulate the truth I will briefly tell them here.

In the first, Faya Feda said there were four people he healed from demon possession but then told me five stories. One story seemed a briefer summation of one of the others so I folded them into one and assumed those were the four.

In the second, Abdisa Duguma said after he had a frightening dream he ran past the Christian funeral on the way to the church and then when he came back home his house was full of ants. I don't know if I heard correctly, or how these related to the story, so I left them out, assuming the main meaning was still preserved.

The third was when Abdisa Duguma told a story about how he discovered his grandpa wasn't an Orthodox priest like he thought, but a witch doctor. I took it out for the lack of miracle and for the sake of space.

The fourth time was when Girma Jabesa Dorsisa told a story in which the wife of a member of another denomation died because they were were debating wrong theology with him. Girma was making the point that God can use suffering to correct our behavior. This one sounds like the ruthlessness often seen in the Old Testament but I think it would really confuse our culture, so I put it back here for anyone really ready to dig in.

The fifth time was several consecutive stories Girma told. One time he was having a Bible study and the mother of one of his students who was practicing witchcraft ran into their room screaming. Another time a woman interrupted a funeral he was leading and he shouted in Jesus' name and she fell down. Another time they were stranded when a river flooded but prayed for help and a man came. They went back with him and his whole house was saved. I didn't think it was important enough for the space it took up.

The sixth was when some people broke the leg of one of his cows but he prayed for it and it got up and went home with him. Then the cow of the person who had broken the leg was hit by a car and killed and he confessed to Girma that he had broken the leg. I didn't think the story demonstrated anything new for the amount of space it took up.

The seventh was when Girma prayed that a man would come back from pursuing school so he could be in the ministry. The man cried "Halleluja" in the middle of one of his classes and couldn't go to school after that until he had become a minister in the church. This is sort of a confusing one for the west because we think education is almost always good. And it didn't add much so I thought I'd just set that can of worms aside.

The eighth was when Tesfaye Haylemarian said there was a person with him when a man came to attack him. He asked the person if he knew who the attacker was. I don't think the answer was reported to me, and I didn't think it contributed to the point of the story either way.

The ninth part was when Tesfaye Haylemarian told me the story of his conversion, which included a vision of Jesus, who told him he didn't have to worship angels anymore. But I didn't think that was an issue Americans dealt with so I left it out. Also in this vision he talks about seeing the Word of God as several books leaning against each other. I refer to this part of the vision later so I move his telling of that part of that vision to that time. He also told a story of coincidental meetings and an unclear healing, neither of which were very compelling, so I left them out.

Also part of his conversion was a story of "dark men" entering his house with their children and the only way of turning them away was to say the name of Jesus, which popped into his head. This seemed like an unclear story that didn't demonstrate very much, so I left it out. And then he told how his wife died and he lost all his crops. No one could help for a long time. I didn't think this added enough value for the space it took up.

The tenth was when he told a story of his crops being saved when others wouldn't give him water, but it was similar to the other story like this.

The eleventh was when Tesfaye Haylemarian healed a woman by casting out a demon and making her stop bleeding, which she had been doing for 5 weeks since giving birth. The result was hard to visually measure so I omitted it.

The twelfth was when his wife went dancing for one of the pagan religion's festivals. He prayed for her to get sick until she came back, and she did. I just thought that such a brief telling of this story would cause theological controversy about causing cruelty or suffering and would be better explained elsewhere.

The thirteenth was when a woman made fun of him and he said if you don't take it back you will die. She died and two men were sent, separately on two occasions but neither of them were able to attack him. One of them received Christ. I thought this story again would bring up questions I wasn't ready to explain.

The fourteenth time was when I asked Tesfaye if he needed prayer for anything. He said pray that his name wouldn't be taken from the book of life. He believed it could be taken. This would be a can of worms to open.

The fifthteenth was when I asked Tesfaye Ejeta if there were ever times that people didn't get healed after he prayed for them. He told a story where a missionary woman was over seas and went mad. He prayed for her over the phone and she was healed. So I moved that story here because the woman was healed, and it didn't answer the question.

The sixteenth time was when Tesfaye Ejeta told a brief story of when his friend's crops had been destroyed and Tesfaye gave him help. I think I might have cut him off with one of my questions, not realizing his story wasn't complete, because now I don't understand why he included it.

In the seventeenth time, Alayu was explaining the reason why Israelites are as violent as the Muslims in regions like Gaza. I removed some sentences that were basically redundant in order to make it a more efficient communication.

Also, I changed a lot of pronouns. It was easy for my translator and I to confuse whether we were speaking for the missionary or about him. So upon editing I made it consistent.

If you want to see the original transcript or to hear my amateur audio recordings, I would like to share them with you. Email me at ross.boone@rawspoon.com.

SPECIAL THANKS TO MY KICKSTARTER SUPPORTERS

who made the finances for this trip and the book possible. You have given me much more than I have returned to you. You have changed my life. So I thank you.

And thank you for those of you who critiqued the first drafts of the book so I could make it what it is today.

Also, big thanks to Pastor Ketsela. Thank you for translating all these stories for me!

Kevin Stender

Paigey Pappanastos

Katherine Dunn

Chris Simpson

Shelley Noeldechen

Ali Fraze

John and Lisa Gebert

Brett Hoover

Rachel Kim

Brandi Lies

Jesse Phillips

Kelly Clark

Aaron Elkins

Josh Gwyn

Chad Glenn

Chris and Michelle Miller

Jordan Foxworthy

Brad Muir

Jefferson Davis

Woody Giles

Juan Yer

Amber Wilburn

The Knowles family

Kate Pak

Tim DeGroot

Philip and Emily Dunlop

Mindy King

Ned Gebert

Forrest Curran

Andy Harper

Kate O'Rourke

Lane Scheiblauer

Kate Scott

Jessica Scott

Nick and Kaleigh Boone

Bobbi Jo Brooks

Brad Mauldin

Michael Stille

Chris Stanton

Amber M. Baylor

Maggi Boone

Dick and Conli Fraze

Christianna Luy

Blake Jankewicz

Jon Martinez

Dalton Walker

Glenna Oakley

Noel Hart

Made in the USA
Monee, IL
05 September 2022

13345404R00115